KU-493-889

DEPARTMENT OF THE ENVIRONMENT

PLANNING RESEARCH PROGRAMME

DEPARTMENT OF TRANSPORT

REDUCING TRANSPORT EMISSIONS THROUGH PLANNING

ECOTEC RESEARCH AND CONSULTING LTD

in association with

TRANSPORTATION PLANNING ASSOCIATES

London : HMSO

© Crown copyright 1993
Applications for reproduction should be made to HMSO
First published 1993
Second impression 1993

ISBN 0 11 752785 8

Other recent Planning Research Programme publications include:

Rates of Urbanisation in England 1981–2001.
ISBN 0 11 752356 9 (1990)

An Examination of the Effects of the Use Classes Order 1987 and the General Development Order 1988.
ISBN 0 11 752413 1 (1991)

Permitted Development Rights for Agriculture.
ISBN 0 11 752414 X (1991)

Evaluating the Low Costs Rural Housing Initiative.
ISBN 0 11 752547 1 (1991)

Housing Land Availability.
ISBN 0 11 752419 0 (1991)

Monitoring Environmental Assessment and Planning.
ISBN 0 11 752436 0 (1991)

Development Plans: A Good Practice Guide.
ISBN 0 11 752689 4 (1992)

Evaluating the Effectiveness of Land Use Planning.
ISBN 0 11 752643 6 (1992)

Land Use Planning Policy and Climate Change.
ISBN 0 11 752587 1 (1992)

National Sample Survey of Vacant Land in Urban Areas of England.
ISBN 0 11 752692 4 (1992)

Planning, Pollution and Waste Management.
ISBN 0 11 752668 1 (1992)

The Effects of Major Out of Town Retail Development.
ISBN 0 11 752631 2 (1992)

The Relationship Between House Prices and Land Supply.
ISBN 0 11 752593 6 (1992)

The Use of Planning Agreements.
ISBN 0 11 752659 2 (1993)

The Effectiveness of Green Belts.
ISBN 0 11 752799 8 (1993)

LEEDS METROPOLITAN
UNIVERSITY LIBRARY
1700900709
B24EV
40084 CP2 2914
LEEDS
DISUD

Cover Photograph: Nigel Young, Redevelopment of Charing Cross
Station, London. Terry Farrell and Company Ltd.

Contents

List Of Tables

List of Figures

Preface and Acknowledgements

This report presents the results of a major study to consider the potential of land-use planning to reduce the rate of growth of transport emissions, in particular CO_2. The study was jointly commissioned by the Department of the Environment and the Department of Transport. The Environment White Paper: This Common Inheritance (1990), identified the need for such research. The work has been undertaken by a study team led by ECOTEC Research and Consulting Ltd, who have worked in association with Transportation Planning Associates.

The study has considered the ways in which planning can influence transport emissions by:

a) reducing the need to travel; and

b) changing modal split towards more emissions-efficient modes.

The ways in which planning can achieve this which have been considered in the study include:

- through influencing the location of development and settlement patterns;

- through influencing the density of development; and

- through influencing the mixture of land uses.

In addition, consideration has been given to how planning, in combination with complementary measures, such as parking policies, park-and-ride schemes, pedestrian priority and traffic calming measures, cycleway provision, and public transport priority measures, can influence travel demand and hence transport emissions.

The study has used a number of different approaches to generate new evidence (case studies, simulations of alternative patterns of development and neighbourhood surveys), as well as drawing on existing literature and studies. The planning policies that emerge as having the potential to reduce transport emissions have also been assessed in terms of their impacts on the achievement of other planning objectives.

The study team are very grateful to the many individuals who have contributed to the work and provided time and information. They are particularly grateful to John ZETTER of DPSI Division of the Department of the Environment and Chairman of the Steering Group for the study, to all members of the Steering Group and the Departments' nominated officers Michael BACH (Department of the Environment) and John LARKINSON (Department of Transport).

v

Executive Summary

1. The report presents the findings of a study to examine the extent to which land-use planning could contribute to reducing travel demand and hence CO_2 emissions. The work was jointly sponsored by the Departments of Environment and Transport and undertaken by ECOTEC Research and Consulting Limited, in association with Transportation Planning Associates. The study uses a range of research techniques: case studies and statistical analyses at the regional and local scale; simulations using existing land-use transportation models; a literature review; and empirical work at the neighbourhood level.

2. Transport accounts directly for approximately 20% of CO_2 emissions in the UK, and the contribution of transport to overall CO_2 emissions and other greenhouse gases has been growing. Road transport, and particularly the private motor car, dominate transport-related CO_2 emissions. The projected increases in car ownership and other social trends, such as the increase in the number of households and participants in the labour market, globalisation of the economy and increasing integration between economic activities, are likely to reinforce tendencies towards growth in travel demand and hence increase CO_2 emissions from transport.

3. In recognition of the problem of global warming the UK Government has signed the Climate Change Convention. This calls for measures to reduce CO_2 emissions to 1990 levels by 2000. If the transport sector is to contribute to this reduction there are three mechanisms through which this could be achieved:

(i) through reductions in overall travel demand;

(ii) through encouraging the use of more emissions-efficient modes of travel; and

(iii) through changes in the emissions efficiency of transport.

This study has examined the contribution that land-use planning could make through, for example, influencing densities, urban structure and facilities at the neighbourhood level, both to reducing overall travel demand and to encouraging the use of more emissions-efficient modes.

Main study findings

4. The main study findings concern the impact of density, settlement size and regional, urban and neighbourhood structures on transport emissions. The study also considers the impact of new transport infrastructure on development pressures.

Density

5. Higher residential densities within settlements are likely to be associated with reductions in travel demand and the encouragement of shifts towards emissions-efficient modes. Determining precisely where key thresholds are is problematic given the existing levels of disaggregation of the available data sources. However, travel demand rises quickly as density falls below 15 persons per hectare and falls sharply as density increases above 50 persons per hectare. Assessing the extent of the reduction in transport emissions which higher densities can achieve is complicated by factors such as the interrelationships between income and density, and possible adaptive responses by home buyers. Simple comparisons between the transport energy efficiency of settlements with different densities provide only a limited guide to the actual level of transport emission reductions which would result from general increases in the density of residential developments (Section 2.2).

Settlement Size

6. The dispersal of population from major centres has been associated with increases in travel demand and a shift away from public transport towards the private motor car. It is also evident that smaller settlements (those with populations of less than 50,000, but particularly very small settlements) are characteristically less transport emissions-efficient than larger settlements. However, the relationships between settlement size and transport emissions are again complicated by other factors, notably differences in levels of car ownership (Section 2.3).

Regional structure

7. The extent of urbanisation within regions is an important determinant of travel demand. Whilst formal proof is difficult, transport emissions are likely to be lower where there is a balance of population, employment and other activities within individual urban areas and a reasonable level of geographic separation between centres (Section 2.4).

Urban structure and centralisation

8. Centralisation of employment and other high travel-generating activities (leisure, retail etc) significantly increase the use of public transport compared to less centralised urban structures. However, high levels of centralisation and concentration of land uses are also associated with longer-distance trips (and hence higher overall levels of travel). The evidence on the effects on travel behaviour of polynuclear (multi-centred) urban structures and the general intermixing of land uses is less clear. Both potentially offer a more transport emissions-efficient urban structure. However, this potential may not be realised in practice (Section 2.4).

Neighbourhood structure

9. A high proportion of all travel is essentially local and a very high proportion of all trips are relatively short. Around 75% of all journeys in Britain are under 8kms in length; half are under 3kms; and 32% are under 1.6kms. This indicates the considerable potential for a shift to more emissions-efficient modes, particularly walking. The review of evidence indicates that proximity to local centres, the choice of available facilities and design characteristics are important factors in encouraging their use. Walking, and to a lesser extent cycling, are important modes for short journeys (Section 2.4).

Responding to the development pressures generated by new transport infrastructure

10. New transport infrastructure can, depending upon existing local planning policies:

*   enable people to extend their housing location search and improve their access to a wider choice of job opportunities;

*   improve the market prospects for development at particular locations: and

*   strongly influence, in the case of orbital road routes, the relative accessibility of peripheral as opposed to central locations.

Each of these impacts can be highly significant in influencing overall transport emissions (Section 2.5). Planning measures, such as the safeguarding of locations with improved road access for land uses having an inherent need for such sites and the concentration of development in locations benefitting from improvements in public transport, are required to minimise potential increases in transport emissions associated with new transport infrastructure (Section 3.2).

Implications for planning

11. The evidence of the study indicates that, in overall terms, the planning policies most pertinent to the objective of reducing travel demand and encouraging use of emissions-efficient modes are:

*   the focusing of development in urban areas;

*   the maintenance and revitalisation of existing neighbourhood, town and city centres; and

*   constraints on the development of small settlements and the extension of villages within the commuter belt.

The study also identifies a range of planning measures pertinent to the different purposes of travel (Section 4.2).

Planning and different travel purposes

12. Reductions in transport emissions from **journeys to or from work** (20% of total car travel in 1985/86) will be encouraged by:

*   the concentration of employment uses in existing centres well served by public transport;

*   high-density residential developments concentrated near to transport nodes and in corridors served by public transport; and

*   the release of adequate housing land, particularly in urban areas, to maximise the possibilities for households to locate close to their places of work.

13. As regard **travel within the course of work** (10% of total travel by car in 1985/86), the above measures need to be complemented by:

*   measures to reinforce urban and city-centre regeneration and to encourage the juxtaposition of the types of economic activity not inherently car dependent; and

- road/rail interchange facilities to encourage people to change to rail for longer-distance journeys.

In addition, measures to keep open and create options for reusing rail access to individual industrial sites and the establishment of intermodal freight terminals, will help create the potential to transfer goods to rail in appropriate cases.

14. The planning policies most pertinent to reducing CO_2 emissions associated with **travel for shopping** and personal business (22% of car kilometerage in 1985/86) are:

- the encouragement of local convenience shopping;
- the maintenance and revitalisation of existing central and suburban shopping centres; and
- the encouragement of in-centre locations for large convenience/foodstores in district centres.

15. Travel for **social, entertainment and holiday** purposes (32% of total car kilometerage in 1985/86) has experienced very considerable growth. Although planning cannot markedly influence the transport emissions associated with these purposes, relevant polices include:

- the location of leisure facilities in centres or other locations with suitable public transport access; and
- the encouragement of local leisure and entertainment facilities.

16. Travel, particularly travel by car for **educational purposes** has also experienced growth. The planning policies that are relevant to reducing transport emissions associated with the use of educational and other public facilities, such as hospitals and local government offices, include:

- ensuring that decisions on the location or relocation of facilities include consideration of the travel demand implications;
- the provision of educational and other public facilities in parallel with residential development; and
- incorporating design characteristics and infrastructure that facilitate the use of emission-efficient modes, including cycling and walking.

Planning and complementary measures

17. Overall planning is likely to have a greater impact on travel demand and the encouragement of

emissions-efficient modes if it is coupled with other complementary measures including: parking controls, park-and-ride schemes, pedestrian priority measures and traffic calming, cycleway provision and public transport priority measures. Planning can also contribute to the success of other measures, such as economic instruments, by facilitating opportunities for travel by emissions-efficient modes (Section 3.3).

Tools to assist the land-use planning process.

18. There are five "tools" that would assist the land-use planning process to generate strategies, plans, policies and measures, which will reduce transport emissions (Section 3.4):

- strategic studies to assess the impacts and costs and benefits of alternative land-use and transport strategies at the regional and county level;
- studies to provide a basis for the co-ordination of land-use and other measures at the urban scale;
- techniques to assess the overall travel, as well as the local traffic impact, of new developments;
- demonstration projects exhibiting the possibilities for high densities of economic activities and households within high-quality urban environments; and,
- the definition of priority zones around new transport infrastructures.

Relationship to current policies

19. There is a good correspondence between the planning policies stressed above and existing planning objectives and measures, even though few planning policies have been pursued with the explicit objective of reducing transport emissions. Furthermore, a systematic assessment of these and other measures which are likely to reduce travel demand reveals that major detrimental impacts on the achievement of existing planning objectives are unlikely (Section 3.2). Indeed, the measures will have benefits in terms of enhancing accessibility for households without cars and improving local environments. The most significant risks are associated with possible increases in congestion.

20. In the pursuit of CO_2 reductions, congestion has possible benefits as a suppressant of demand - particularly if good quality public transport alternatives are available. However, it involves costs associated with the CO_2 inefficiency of vehicles in congested con-

ditions and with rerouting by vehicles seeking to avoid congested areas. Improvements in engine-management technologies could reduce the importance of the CO_2 costs associated with lower operating inefficiencies in congested urban areas. Reducing urban congestion would require complementary policies.

Scope for change

21.   The rate of change of land uses is relatively slow; overall the built fabric is renewed at only about 1-2% per annum, although some high travel generating land uses are renewed more quickly. The UK is comparatively densely populated with a stable urban structure and travel demand is on a par with the European average. These two factors limit the extent to which planning in the UK can impact upon transport emissions. Certainly the potential to reduce transport emissions varies between areas and depends upon local circumstances. However, the evidence of this report points to planning measures over time achieving a significant impact on transport emissions. One of the simulations undertaken in the study indicated that planning policies in combination with transport measures could reduce projected transport emissions by 16% over a 20-year period. These findings are similar to those of other work which indicates that 10-15% savings in fuel usage, and hence emissions, from passenger transport might be achieved through land-use changes at the city region scale over a 25-year period (Section 1.4). Further emphasis on the planning policies, in combination with complementary and transport measures stressed above, therefore seems justified in the light of the possible long-term consequences of global warming and the associated improvement in the urban environment that could be achieved through these planning measures.

Priorities for further research

22.   There remain many areas of uncertainty concerning the complex relationships between land uses that can be influenced by planning and their impact upon travel demand. The analysis has also been constrained by the lack of availability of suitable and up-to-date data. There are several areas where focused research would be of benefit to inform the questions addressed in this study and the policies put forward (Section 4.3). These include :

- assessment of the changes in travel behaviour of individuals and households resulting from changes in place of residence and place of work;

- research into the type of travel demand generated by emergent land uses;

- research on short-distance trips;

- further analyses of the relationship between density, settlement size and regional, urban and neighbourhood structure on transport emissions;

- assessments of the implications of intensification and centralisation on travel patterns;

- assessments of the implications of developing local facilities;

- assessments of the effects of complementary measures on transport emissions;

- research into the effects of locating offices and employment uses near to public transport facilities;

- research into the adaptability of planning measures to technological changes which affect transport emissions;

- predicting and monitoring of the impact on travel demand and modal choice of co-ordinated planning and transport strategies; and

- ex-post, longitudinal assessments of the development and travel impacts of major road and rail projects.

Part I Introduction and Context

1.1 The Scope of the Study

Introduction

1.1.1   This report presents the findings of a study to examine the extent to which land-use planning can contribute to reducing the rate of growth of travel demand and hence carbon dioxide (CO_2) emissions. The work was jointly commissioned by the Departments of the Environment and Transport and undertaken by ECOTEC Research and Consulting Limited, in association with Transportation Planning Associates.

1.1.2   In September 1990 the UK Government published an Environment White Paper - 'This Common Inheritance' - which committed the Government to reducing the upward trend of CO_2 emissions, provided that other countries take similar action.[1] It also identified the need for research to investigate the relationship between land use patterns and travel demand. In June 1992 the Government signed the Climate Change Convention which commits the UK to reducing CO_2 emissions to 1990 levels by 2000.[2]

1.1.3   Transport accounts for approximately 20% of CO_2 emissions in the UK, a figure which rises to 23% when emissions from refineries associated with the production of fuel for vehicles are taken into account. The contribution of transport to overall CO_2 emissions and other greenhouse gases has been growing over time, both in relative and absolute terms. Road transport, and particularly the private motor car, dominate transport-related CO_2 emissions. The predicted increase in car ownership and other social trends, such as the growth in the number of households and increasing integration between economic activities, are likely to reinforce tendencies towards growth in travel demand and, hence, CO_2 emissions from transport. Land-use planning policies that lessen the propensity to travel and provide the opportunity of using emissions-efficient modes would clearly contribute to a reduction of the rate of growth of CO_2 emissions. Such measures could also significantly contribute to a lessening of other adverse environmental impacts of transport (eg. noise and carbon monoxide emissions).

1.1.4   It is necessary to consider the potential impact of land use planning measures from a long-term perspective. Whilst the need for immediate action to reduce emissions is widely acknowledged, there are uncertainties over the timing and character of global warming. Land uses change relatively slowly, at an overall rate of perhaps 1-2% per annum, although some significant travel-generating land uses are renewed more quickly. Thus, land-use planning cannot promote rapid changes in overall settlement patterns. However, it can powerfully influence the location of particular land uses - including major travel-generating uses, such as retailing and leisure developments - and, hence, the extent to which accessibility to facilities is dependent on the use of private cars.

1.1.5   There are likely to be technological responses to the problem of transport emissions, particularly through steady increases in the fuel efficiency of new vehicles. However, such improvements will take time before they impact markedly upon the overall efficiency of the vehicle stock. Furthermore, the emissions consequences of such improvements are likely to be offset by the anticipated growth in vehicle use.

1.1.6   There are also close interlinkages between land-use planning and transport policy issues. The provision of transport infrastructure influences accessibility and the relative attractiveness of different locations. The availability of public transport, which is in general terms more emissions-efficient than private transport, strongly influences the potential of planning to influence modal choice. At the same time, planning measures can increase urban densities and, thus, influence the viability of public transport, as well as encouraging walking and cycling. Planning can also influence the extent to which travel demand is focused within confined areas. This has implications for congestion which also, in turn, influences travel behaviour. The focus of this study is on the role which land-use planning can play in reducing travel-related CO_2 emissions. The extent to which planning policies can support other CO_2 emissions reduction measures is also considered.

1.1.7   Economic instruments, such as road pricing, carbon taxes, and other legislative measures, can have important impacts upon travel demand and modal choice and, thus, CO_2 emissions. Such measures are not the focus of this study. However, if the planning measures put forward precede other policy measures - or external events - that effectively increase the real cost of travel by private car, these planning measures will enable more travel-related needs to be satisfactorily met in the longer term, for a given cost, than would otherwise be the case. Thus, in addition to the immediate environmental, economic and accessibility benefits of reducing travel demand, much of the rationale for introducing the land-use planning measures put forward in this report rests upon the need for contingency planning; to be ready for circumstances in which the urgency of global warming, intolerable levels of congestion and urban environmental stress may require transport demand to be reduced by other means. The policies are generally in line with existing planning policies so that, in the event that such action to reduce CO_2 levels from transport does not prove necessary, little will have been lost.

Objectives and key questions

1.1.8   The specific objectives of the study were to:

(a)   collect information on and review current knowledge of the relationship between settlement patterns, land uses, and travel demand;

(b)   identify the extent to which planning policies can influence travel demand and modal choice;

(c)   consider the impact of transport provision on settlement, development and travel patterns; and

(d)   consider the contribution different planning measures can make to reducing travel demand and CO_2 emissions.

1.1.9   In meeting these objectives the study has addressed the following key questions raised by the study brief:

- What are the current patterns and recent trends in travel generated by particular types of settlement patterns and land uses?

- How do current planning policies and development trends influence the demand for travel?

- What impacts do new transport projects have on settlement, development and travel patterns?

- What are the likely limitations on the effectiveness of planning policies and what conflicts might arise with other planning objectives?

1.1.10   In addressing these questions the study has explored the ways in which planning can influence transport emissions by:

- reducing the need to travel; and

- encouraging the choice of more emissions-efficient or non-polluting modes.

Planning could achieve this through influencing: the density of development and population; the size of settlements; and the structure of urban areas and settlement patterns within regions. The evidence indicating the likely influence of planning in each of these respects is reviewed in Part II. In addition, the study has considered the effects of transport infrastructure on development pressures and the consequent land-use planning responses that could help reduce transport emissions.

Method of approach

1.1.11   The method of approach adopted by the study consisted of five elements which are outlined below.

(i) A review of previous research

1.1.12   This was based upon a review of data and literature concerning the analysis of travel patterns, purposes and development trends; empirical and ex-post evaluations of land-use and transport studies; urban freight movements and environmental conditions; and the relationship between CO_2 emissions and distance travelled by vehicle type, and the impact on these relationships on factors such as speed and congestion. This review also included overall assessments of recent, current and likely future trends in settlement patterns and in the location of specific travel-generating uses, and the effectiveness of the planning system in influencing land-use and travel patterns.

(ii) Case studies: longitudinal and cross-sectional analyses

1.1.13 Regions, urban areas and neighbourhoods which exhibit a variety of settlement/land-use configurations and types of transport provision were chosen as case studies The case study areas are listed in Appendix 3. The evidence assembled on land-use patterns and travel demand was used both to inform analyses of the relationship between settlement characteristics (density, size, etc.) and travel demand, and to provide illustrations of the potential influence of particular planning measures. The data, in particular, enabled a range of statistical analyses of the factors influencing travel demand, and facilitated considerations of particular planning issues. The work was further informed by the review of some specific land-use planning and related measures which have been implemented in other UK and continental European cities.

(iii) Simulations of alternative patterns of development

1.1.14 For a subset of the case study areas, strategic land-use and transportation planning models were used to simulate the implications for travel demand of alternative spatial patterns of possible future growth, and of alternative locations for major trip attracting activities.

(iv) Supplementary surveys

1.1.15 The work was also informed by the findings of recent studies examining the travel-generation characteristics of new and contrasting developments. In addition, and in order to fill gaps in existing knowledge, empirical work was undertaken at the neighbourhood level. This comprised household questionnaire surveys (from which some 1,300 returns in total were achieved), complemented by surveys of local facilities.

(v) Consultations

1.1.16 Discussions were held with a range of planning and transport authorities to establish their views on the ways in which land use changes, new transport infrastructure and local trends in transport demand have interacted in the case study areas; to identify aspects of the local planning policy context; and to secure relevant data not held by the study team. In addition, a number of consultations were held with national organisations.

1.1.17 In the light of the evidence drawn from these sources, a range of possible planning measures emerged which were assessed systematically within a consistent analytical framework. This framework took account of: likely impact on aspects of travel demand; dependence on supportive policies; implications for other publicly-borne costs; costs and benefits to different groups; major risks and uncertainties involved; and contributions to the achievement of other planning and public policy objectives.

1.1.18 An advisory panel, comprising senior members of ECOTEC and Transportation Planning Associates and invited specialists, was established to comment on the study methodology, on key assumptions underpinning the analytical work and the emerging conclusions from the study.

Structure of the Report

1.1.19 Part II of this report draws together the main study findings concerning the relationship between land uses, transport infrastructure and travel behaviour. Part III considers the relevance of these findings to planning. It also assesses the likely effectiveness of planning policies and considers the role of complementary policies. Part IV provides the study's conclusions and priorities for future research. The remainder of Part I provides a context for the study findings.

1.1.20 The report contains four Appendices: Appendix 1 provides further detail on the results of the simulation studies; Appendix 2 assesses a number of planning policy options, which would help achieve the objective of reducing transport emissions, against a range of criteria; Appendix 3 provides a list of the case study areas; and Appendix 4 describes the statistical analysis of the determinants of travel demand in Great Britain undertaken in the study.

1.2 Key Trends in Travel Behaviour and Land Use Patterns

Introduction

1.2.1 This section of the report reviews evidence on trends in travel purpose and trip patterns and on the predicted growth in travel demand. It then considers some of the main patterns of land-use change and the factors underpinning both changes in land-use patterns and travel behaviour.

Trends in travel purposes and trip patterns

1.2.2 Figure 1 indicates key changes in travel demand over the period 1965 to 1986 from the National Travel Survey (NTS). There has been a steady and large increase in overall distance travelled per person per week. The numbers of journeys have not increased markedly, and actually experienced some decline in the period 1979 to 1986. But in terms of total distance travelled this decline was more than offset by an increase in average journey lengths.

1.2.3 Figure 2(a) indicates the relative importance of different purposes of car kilometerage in 1985/6, and Figure 2(b) shows the contribution of each trip type to the growth in car travel experienced between 1978/79 and 1985/6. The following overall observations can be made:

- social and entertainment purposes (32% of all car travel), shopping and personal business (22%), and journeys to and from work (20%) are the most important car travel purposes;

- three trip purposes experienced particularly high rates of growth over the period 1978/9 - 1985/86. Holidays and day trips increased by 362%, social and entertainment by 314% and travel in the course of work by 212%; and

- social and entertainment trips accounted for 35% of the total growth in travel by car over this period; holiday and day trips accounted for 21% of total growth and journeys to and from work for 18%.

1.2.4 In 1985/86 car travel accounted for 69% of all journeys of more than 1.6km (42% as driver and 27% as passenger). Comparing NTS data for 1978/9 and 1985/6 indicates that:

- the average number of weekly journeys undertaken by car increased by 6.5%. The average number of journeys by car passengers decreased for all purposes; and

- average car journey lengths increased for all purposes by 51% and this was the overriding reason for the overall increase in vehicle kilometerage.

B

Figure 1: **Travel Trends 1965–1986**

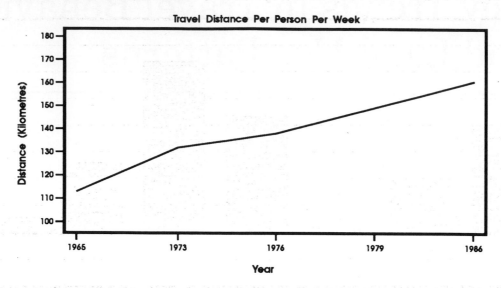

Travel Distance Per Person Per Week

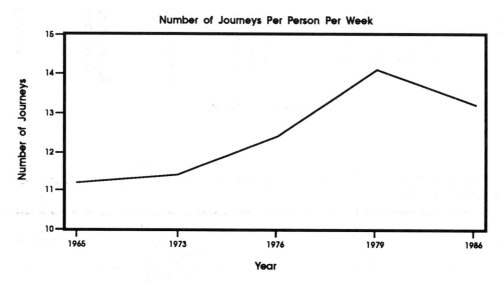

Number of Journeys Per Person Per Week

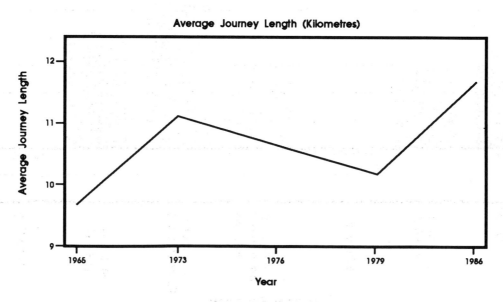

Average Journey Length (Kilometres)

Notes: Figures include all journeys above 1.6 km by
car, local bus, rail, walk and other (2 wheel, taxi, etc)

Source: National Travel Survey.

Figure 2a: **Analysis of Car Travel by Journey Purpose for 1985–86**

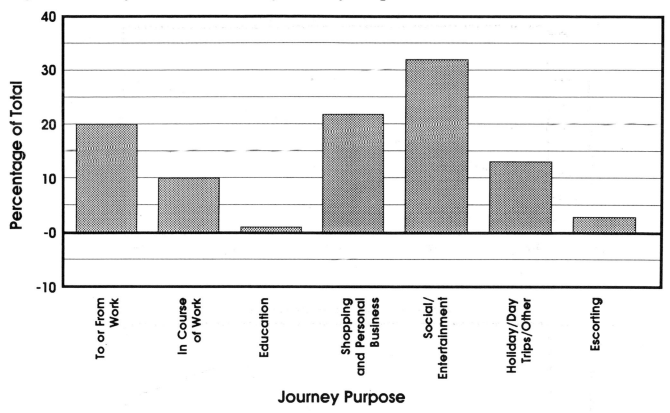

Figure 2b: **The Contribution to the Growth in Car Travel by Journey Purpose: 1978–79—1985–86**

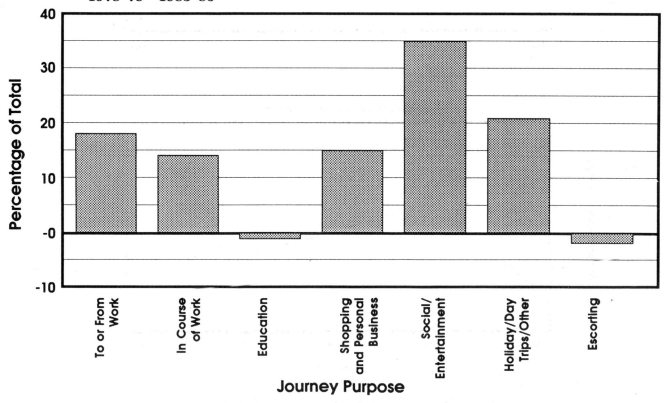

Source: National Travel Surveys 1979 and 1986.

Notes: *The term escorting is applied when the traveller has no purpose of his/her own other than to escort or accompany another person, for example taking a child to school.*

1.2.5 The characteristics of travel for different purposes are briefly reviewed below.

Journeys to or from work

1.2.6 Journeys to or from work accounted for 20% of total travel by car in 1985/86. As Table 1 shows, car use accounted for nearly two-thirds of total travel by all modes for this journey purpose, although travel by train was also significant. Considerable absolute growth took place over the period 1978/79 to 1985/86, but the relative contribution of this travel purpose to CO_2 emissions has probably not increased. For the future, factors such as specialisation in the labour market may, as discussed below, continue to increase journey-to-work travel, but it is unlikely that overall travel to work will increase in future as quickly as travel demand as a whole. Consideration has also been given to the extent to which telematics might reduce the frequency and length of journeys to work. However, there is little evidence to suggest that marked general reductions are likely in the immediate future.

Other work-related travel

1.2.7 Motorised forms of transport are a dominant proportion of travel in the course of work. It accounted for 10% of passenger car kilometres in 1985/6 and trends, such as increasing economic integration, the separation of service activities from manufacturing, and more flexibility of work organisation, suggest that this source of travel demand is likely to increase.

Shopping and personal business

1.2.8 Travel for shopping and personal business accounted for 22% of car kilometerage in 1985/86. Table 1 shows that walking and bus are important modes for this purpose, accounting for one-fifth of kilometerage travelled. The amount of travel has been increasing, but at a lower rate than overall travel demand. Cars have increased their share of shopping journeys (between 1972/73 and 1978/79 the share increased from 27% to 32%) and journeys have lengthened.[3] These trends have been associated with:

- increases in total retail floorspace (although consumer expenditure has increased more rapidly);

- concentration of floorspace in larger and fewer retail units; and

- increasing car ownership and the increased mobility of women in particular.

1.2.9 The scale, type and location of retail developments have implications for the types of trips attracted, as well as for their length and mode. The following observations can be made:

- Entirely new trips generated by retail developments form a small proportion of all trips (around 5%). Multi-purpose or "diverted" trips account for around 40% of all trips. Thus, the majority of trips tend to be transfers from other destinations and "pass-by" trips. The latter do not lead to additional travel demand; and

Table 1 : **Percentage of Total Travel by Different Modes According to Journey Purpose: 1985/86**

(km)

Trip Purpose / Mode	To/ From Work	In course of work	Education	Shopping & personal business	Eat/drink entertainment & sport	Visit friends & Social	Holidays & Day Trips	Escorting	Total 1985 /86	Comparison with NTS 1975
Walk	3	1	15	10	5	3	5	5	5	6
Bicycle	2	–	3	1	1	–	1	–	1	1
Motorcycle	2	–	1	1	1	1	1	–	1	1
Car	64	74	29	71	76	80	66	86	71	71
Van/lorry	8	18	1	2	2	2	1	2	4	–
Local Bus	7	–	21	10	4	5	1	3	6	9
Coach/Express bus	–	–	1	–	1	2	5	–	1	2
Taxi/Minicab	–	–	1	–	1	1	–	–	1	1
Train	12	5	7	3	3	5	6	2	6	7
Private hire/ Tour bus	–	1	21	1	5	1	12	1	3	2
Other transport modes	1	2	–	1	1	–	2	1	1	–
Total	100	100	100	100	100	100	100	100	100	100

Source: National Travel Survey 1985/86 & Vital Travel Statistics, 1979 & 1983 edition.

Note :   NTS figures for 1975 do not include a separate breakdown for the Van/lorry category.

            These data exclude trips under 1.6 km. If short trips were included, the proportion of trips in which people walked would be greater.

- The number of pass-by trips tends to decrease with increasing shopping centre size; the large centres also tend to attract "weekly" car-borne shoppers.[4]

Travel for social and entertainment purposes

1.2.10 Travel for social and entertainment purposes is dominated by car journeys and accounted for 32% of total car kilometerage in 1985/86. It also accounted for 35% of the overall increase in travel demand during the period 1978/79 to 1985/86. This increase can be linked to general increases in car ownership and wealth. It may also be linked to increasing levels of geographical mobility within the labour market - friends and relatives are consequently more dispersed - and the greater time and resources available for leisure activities, particularly amongst single person households and the "young" retired who have increased in numbers and levels of mobility. Travel demand for this purpose is extremely diverse. For example, the Department of Employment's Leisure Day Visits Survey identifies 30 trip purposes.[5] The largest categories are visiting or meeting friends and relatives (22 %) and visiting a public house or wine bar (11 %). Households with a car available made 80 % of their leisure trips by car. In overall terms, the average distance travelled for leisure trips was almost 48 km and 8 % of trips were over 160 km.

Travel for holidays

1.2.11 Travel for holidays and day-trip purposes accounted for 13% of car kilometerage in 1985/86. It was this travel purpose that experienced the greatest growth between 1978/79 and 1985/86. It is reasonable to assume that continued increases are likely in circumstances of economic growth and low real costs of transport.

Education

1.2.12 Walking, cycling and bus travel account for a significant proportion of total distance travelled for educational purposes (Table 1). Car kilometerage for this purpose accounted for only 1% of total car kilometerage in 1985/6. Longer-term growth of this type of travel is associated with concerns over safety and security. Growth has probably also occurred because of the extension of parental choice towards schooling, encouraging longer journeys to school that cannot easily be undertaken by walking or cycling.

1.2.13 National Travel Survey data shows that the proportion of children among all pedestrian and cyclists killed or seriously injured is much higher than their proportion in the general population. A recent study of children's independent mobility confirms that, with respect to coming home from school, the primary concern of parents is the danger posed by road traffic.[6] Replicating surveys in Germany, the study found that, despite, for example, cycle ownership being higher amongst English children, a larger proportion of German children cycle to school. Nearly a third of the English children were collected from school by car, almost four times the proportion of German children. Pedestrian fatality rates among German children were also lower than among English children.

The UK's comparative travel behaviour

1.2.14 It is important to stress that the UK does not, in the international context, exhibit extremes of travel behaviour. The NTS for 1985/86 indicates that the average distance travelled per capita was approximately 8,300 kilometres per annum, about 70% or 5,800 kilometres of which was by car. The latter figure is very close to the observed average of 5,672 passenger kilometres per capita for 12 European cities in 1980. The average for 10 US cities was 12,029 passenger kilometres per capita, over twice the average for the European cities for which data were assembled. At the other extreme, Tokyo, Singapore and Hong Kong each had an average total distance travelled by car per capita considerably below European levels.[7]

1.2.15 It is also possible to draw some broad comparisons of travel demand in the UK and other major industrialised countries. Statistics are available from international publications, although such comparisons need to be treated with caution because of the differences in the methods of estimation used.

1.2.16 International comparisons for 1990 indicate that average distance travelled per capita was 11,997 kilometres per annum for Great Britain. This figure is similar to that for many other European countries, including France (12,274 kms), Germany (10,983 kms) and Italy (10,815 kms). The average distance travelled per capita per annum in the USA (17,243 kms) is higher, and that for Japan (8,272 kms) considerably below, European levels.[8]

1.2.17 However, the increase in travel demand met by car, over the period 1980 to 1990, has been larger in Great Britain than in other European countries. Thus, by 1990, the average passenger kilometres travelled by car per capita per annum in Great Britain, was the highest in the European Community. Conversely, the proportion of travel demand met by public transport in Great Britain, relative to other European Countries, was low. These comparisons suggest that the scope for reducing overall travel demand may be limited. There may, however, be greater potential to increase the proportion of travel demand met by public transport in Great Britain.

Predicted growth in travel demand

1.2.18   In the absence of major changes in policy and/or fuel prices it is predicted that travel demand will continue to increase. For example, the current National Road Traffic Forecasts (NRTF) predict that, compared to 1988, total road traffic in Great Britain would increase by 83% by 2025 on a low-growth assumption and by 142% on a high-growth assumption. These forecasts are illustrated in Figure 3.

1.2.19   The future growth which is predicted is, in percentage terms, lower than that which occurred in the period 1952 to 1988. Currently, car ownership in Britain is around 330 cars per 1000 persons. Other countries with higher income per capita have higher levels of car ownership as well as more passenger vehicles per road kilometre. It is considered that 'saturation' levels may be as high as 650 cars per 1000 persons, nearly double present levels of car ownership.[9]

Figure 3: **National Road Traffic Forecast: High and Low Scenarios**

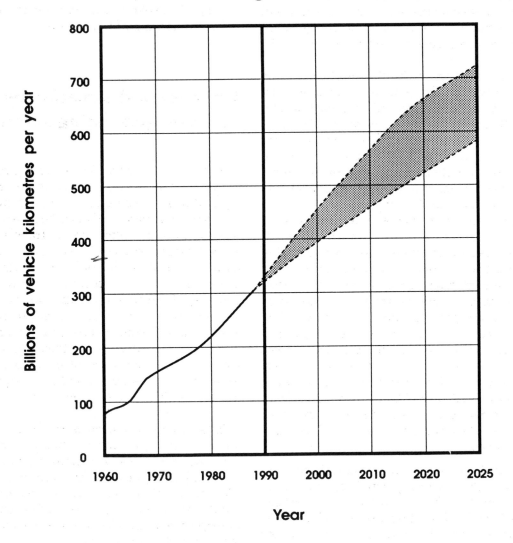

Source: Department of Transport, Road Traffic Forecasts, 1989.

1.2.20 It is likely, therefore, that CO_2 emissions from road transport will rise. Estimates by the Department of Energy anticipate that CO_2 emissions from transport will increase by between 80% and 93% by the year 2020.[10] Independent projections for future CO_2 emissions - such as those prepared by the Earth Resources Research emissions model - estimate that NRTF projections could produce increases in CO_2 emissions of between 60% and 120% from road traffic, even with an assumed average increase in fuel efficiency of cars of around one third over the period.[11]

Patterns of Urban and Regional Growth and Decline

1.2.21 The urban life-cycle model identifies distinct phases of urban development and provides a useful framework within which to consider some of the major trends which have a bearing on travel behaviour.[12]

- **Urbanisation and Suburbanisation** - The industrial revolution brought about a major redistribution of population as industrialisation and urbanisation proceeded hand in hand. The introduction of mass transit systems from the latter part of the nineteenth century onwards increasingly allowed people to live at greater distances from their workplace, permitting the phenomenon of suburbanisation and falling residential densities in the inner areas of cities, such as London.[13] The initial spread of suburban development focused around rail stations. The development of road-based travel - bus, tram and, later in the inter-war period, growing car ownership - allowed growth to spread along the main radial corridors - producing the phenomenon of ribbon development. As transport networks developed, particularly with the advent of wider private car transport in the post-war period and ribbon development was constrained, increasing infilling between these 'ribbons' took place. The post-war period also saw major planned decentralisation in many regions, including the development of new and expanded towns.

- **Counter-urbanisation** - More recently the continuing decentralisation of activities and people from many parts of the main urban areas has been associated with the phenomenon of counter-urbanisation - the declining population of the largest cities and industrial conurbations since the 1970s and the associated population growth in small and medium-sized settlements. This has produced an inverse relationship between population change and settlement size.[14] It has been accompanied by a sharp decline in manufacturing employment in the main conurbations and the growth in smaller towns in rural locations.

- **Reurbanisation** - According to some commentators, the process of counter-urbanisation has now slowed, possibly reflecting the success of urban regeneration measures.[15] However, there is little evidence that market forces alone would produce any more general turnaround as suggested by the life-cycle model.

1.2.22 The evidence on the relative scale and composition of travel generated by different sizes and densities of area, discussed in Part II, suggests that the patterns of urban and regional change identified above have contributed both to the growth in travel demand and to car use. Changes in transport infrastructure and costs have facilitated these spatial changes, although the precise connection between transport developments and, for example, counter-urbanisation is difficult to prove.

Changes in the spatial distribution of travel-generating activities

1.2.23 At the urban level the decentralisation of many of the activities traditionally located in and around urban centres is having a profound effect on the spatial structure of most large towns and cities, with important implications for travel behaviour. Key causal factors involved here include: the reduced importance of agglomeration economies to many activities and the increasing importance of the diseconomies of congestion in urban areas; the search for greater and lower-cost space; the process of activities seeking to follow the outward movement of their customers and workforces; and the better accessibility in peripheral locations provided by the combination of rising car ownership, links to orbital and inter-urban routes and high levels of car parking.

1.2.24 There has been a move away from many urban centres of major publicly-provided facilities over the past decade. For example, the reorganisation of local health facilities has frequently involved the closure of both local and older centrally-located hospitals in favour of edge-of-town developments. Other important aspects of this process over the past decade have included the following:

- **Business parks** - the growth of business parks has been associated with a shift by particular service activities from central to peripheral locations. In terms of travel demand, the majority of companies moving to out-of-town locations tend to be those with a high proportion of professional staff with their own transport, who gain most from the peripheral locations and the ready availability of parking on most such developments. Evidence suggests that their level of car dependence is very high - most business parks tend to be relatively isolated and remote from public transport links and potential sources of labour supply.[16]

- **Retail parks** - a particularly strong locational trend during the 1980s has been the establishment of groups of large retail outlets on retail parks. These schemes, usually suburban or located at the edge of towns, bring together several types of superstore which share some aspects of infrastructure, such as parking. Most of the early schemes have involved food, DIY, electrical goods and furnishing - often termed 'bulky item superstores' - where shopping by car allows easier customer transport of purchases. A related trend has been towards the establishment of major suburban supermarkets with extensive parking provision - often out-of-centre - and, as a result, largely dependent on car access.

- **Out-of-town shopping centres** - a further related trend has been the development of new centres, such as Meadowhall in Sheffield, serving a wide catchment area and offering a single covered site with a range of services. These developments tend to be designed on a single floor level and take up large areas of land, typically requiring a peripheral and/or greenfield location. Sites are frequently located near motorway junctions, provide extensive car parking and cater for a largely car-borne clientele drawn from a wide area.

- **Leisure and recreation facilities** - the last decade or so has seen the development of major car-dependent leisure facilities away from existing urban centres. Examples include the leisure facilities associated with the out-of-town retail centres, as well as theme parks and multiplex cinemas. Some of the sporting and recreational facilities, such as golf, which have become increasingly popular, by their nature also require suburban or non-urban locations.

1.2.25 Whilst, as indicated, some of these decentralisation pressures are a reflection of the requirement of particular activities for large sites, it is evident that other factors are involved. Rental levels on peripheral business parks are often comparable to or above those in central business district and suburban centres. In the case of the West Midlands, for example, typical rentals per square metre on business park locations around the M42 are comparable to Birmingham City Centre and Solihull centre levels, and are well above those in centres, such as Coventry

and Wolverhampton.[17] This is reflected in the strong continuing interest by developers in peripheral sites, even in the current market climate.

1.2.26 It is possible to overstate these pressures. Many city centres retain a strong position in the retailing hierarchy for comparison shopping. Equally, a range of office activities still demand a central location because of the need for interaction with contacts in related businesses (for example, in many financial services), the need to be accessible to customers (for example, retail banks and property agents) or dependence on a workforce with limited car ownership (for example, many administrative functions).

Key socio-economic factors influencing land use and travel demand

1.2.27 Much of the growth in personal and business travel, and many of the land use changes discussed above, are associated with significant changes in the structure and functioning of the UK economy and/or with pervasive social and lifestyle trends. The key factors involved are reviewed below.

Economic trends

1.2.28 Key trends include:

- **Specialisation and economic integration** - one of the key characteristics of economic development is the increase in specialisation which has powerful impacts on travel. Growth tends to increase the volume of goods to be moved and attempts to realise scale economies in the manufacturing sector involve the concentration of production, increasing the separation of production from final markets.[18] Economic growth and the Single European Market mean that this trend is likely to continue for the foreseeable future. Similarly, the evolution of more specialised workforce skills leads to a widening of areas of job search and tends to increase average journey-to-work lengths;

- **Manufacturing technology** - the development of 'just-in-time' methods - whereby firms operate with a minimum level of stock, drawing in supplies as and when needed from a network of suppliers - leads to smaller and more frequent shipments.[19] Although currently limited, the use of such methods is likely to grow in many sectors as European manufacturers seek to compete with the Japanese who have been in the forefront of such developments;

- **Economies of agglomeration** - transportation improvements and new communications technologies are an important factor in permitting the spatial separation of activities from their markets and suppliers. The economies of agglomeration in urban areas for manufacturing activities in particular have clearly been reduced over time, whilst the diseconomies of an urban location in terms of congestion-related costs have increased. In combination with the physical constraints of locations in older urban areas, this has almost certainly contributed to the well-documented urban/rural shift in manufacturing employment; [20]

- **Growth of the services sector** - the most important structural change in the UK and other developed economies has been the growth in the service sector. The nature of many service activities involves work or non-work travel to bring supplier and customer into contact;

- **Externalisation of services** - since the mid 1970s there has been a tendency for manufacturing to buy in from outside various corporate services, previously provided 'in-house', in order to lower costs. [21] These changes in organisation have contributed to the increases in work-related travel by separating the users and providers of the services concerned;

- **Communications technology** - the development of new office equipment and improved data transmission networks make it possible to separate 'back-office' functions from central management activities. [22] This has enabled the decentralisation and dispersal of office employment from the major urban areas, particularly London, again increasing the need for in-work travel; and

- **Public service provision** - for a range of publicly-provided services - such as hospitals - there has been a tendency to seek to realise economies of scale by concentrating facilities in fewer, larger centres. There has also been a trend to select non-central locations where large sites are easier to obtain and costs to the service provider may be lower. This has reduced the range of local facilities within walking distance or easily accessible by public transport, and increased the need for motorised travel in general and car travel in particular.

Social and lifestyle factors

1.2.29 Key factors include:

- **Rising car ownership** - higher levels of car ownership - encouraged by higher real incomes - are associated with an increase in mobility, higher trips rates, increased car use, increased trip lengths and more multi-purpose trips. [23] They have, more generally, reduced the traditional ties linking places of residence, work and other activities;

- **Income and lifestyle** - increasing incomes and leisure time are important influences on travel behaviour. A significant factor is the exercise of choice as people are able, and choose, not to use the nearest opportunity for a range of particular activities from education, to leisure and shopping. Analogous behaviour is also evident in residential preferences, where people have become increasingly willing to travel greater distances in order to satisfy their aspirations for improved housing and space. This is reflected in the strong demand for low-density detached housing in rural areas. Higher incomes have also been associated with a substantial widening of the personal horizons of much of the population with important implications for holiday and other forms of personal travel;

- **Activity rates** - the growth in economic activity rates amongst women has clearly contributed to the observed increase in the number of work-related trips. [24] It is also influencing the nature of households' residential location and travel decisions and is having powerful effects on shopping and other non-work travel behaviour;

- **Demographic factors and life cycles** - analyses of urban household travel behaviour suggest a marked association between life-cycle stages and travel patterns, indicating that changes in the structure of the population and households have significant implications for travel demand. For example, the rise in the number of single-person households and young couples without children is almost certainly associated with an increase in the number of social and recreation trips as these groups tend to show greater participation rates in leisure activities. [25] More generally, the increase in the level of geographical mobility within the labour market means that friends and relatives are more widely dispersed. Time and resources - particularly for leisure activities - have also increased, especially for groups such as the "young" retired. Conversely, for the future, the increased number of households consisting of older people with reduced levels of mobility may be associated with both changes in travel behaviour and a wish to locate closer to facilities; and

- **Consumer technologies** - home appliances, such as washing machines, driers, dishwashers, refrigerators and freezers, are now common in many homes. Freezers are one of the more significant consumer innovations and are associated with an increase in bulk-buying and changes in consumer behaviour to which the major retailers have both contributed and responded. Home entertainment has changed drastically with the diffusion of new forms of consumer electronic equipment, such as video cassette recorders and home computers. The impact of such innovations is as yet difficult to assess because of the lack of data. However, evidence from the United States suggests that "home-based leisure" activities may be reducing the number of social/recreation trips which are made during the evening.[26]

1.2.30 Thus, a wide range of economic and social changes, together with technological developments are combining to widen the areas over which people and businesses conduct their activities, with significant direct implications for travel demand. These same changes are also in many cases, as discussed above, contributing to the observed weakening of the traditional structure of urban areas through reducing the advantages of the centralisation of services, such as retailing, and permitting the wider dispersion and spatial separation of activities. It is this second aspect, with its indirect implications for travel behaviour, which provides a potential point of influence for the planning system.

1.2.31 The background trends which are identified are not, of course, immutable. For example, the rate of growth of car ownership and female activity rates may tend to slow as "saturation rates" are reached.[27] The increase in the number of elderly people with limited mobility will also increase the attractiveness of some locations with good access to public facilities. However, many of the trends and changes identified still appear to have some way to go and policies will need to recognise this context.

Summary

1.2.32 In summary, the key trends in travel behaviour and land-use patterns are that:

- there has been a steady and large increase in overall distance travelled per person per week over the period 1965 to 1985 from 113km to 161km (1.2.2);

- three trip purposes experienced particularly high rates of growth in recent years: holiday and day trips, social and entertainment trips, and travel during the course of work (1.2.3);

- whilst the average number of weekly journeys undertaken by car rose only marginally, there was a 51% increase in average car journey lengths for all purposes over the period 1978/9 to 1985/6. This has been the principal reason for the increase in vehicle kilometerage(1.2.4);

- the average distance travelled per capita in the UK is on a par with the average for European countries. The European average is itself between those for per capita travel in North America and Asia (1.2.14);

- the current NRTF predicts that, compared with 1988, total road traffic in Great Britain will increase by between 83% and 142% (1.2.18). It has been estimated that this would produce an increase in CO_2 emissions from transport of between 60% and 120% by the year 2025;

- the processes of urbanisation and suburbanisation, counterurbanisation and decentralisation, and reurbanisation have been influenced by the availability of private motor transport and, in turn, have influenced travel demand (1.2.21);

- individual land uses which are often located on sites outside of urban centres and which are associated with high levels of car usage have increased in importance (1.2.24); and

- a range of economic and social changes have, and are continuing to, increase directly the demand for travel noted above. Many of these same changes are implicated in the wider erosion of the forces underpinning the structure of the UK's major urban areas. The consequential decentralisation and spatial separation of activities is an important indirect contributor to the observed growth in travel demand (1.2.28-1.2.31).

1.3 Transport Emissions and the Environment

Introduction

1.3.1 This section considers the contributors to global warming and the relative role played by transport emissions in the UK. Transport is also the source of other pollutants of concern which are discussed below.

Global warming and emissions

1.3.2 The 'greenhouse' effect has emerged as one of the most important international environmental issues. Although considerable uncertainty still surrounds the magnitude and timing of future changes, some consensus has emerged that global climate change is occurring, with possible profound implications for agriculture, natural ecosystems and low-lying coastal areas.[28]

1.3.3 The work of the Inter-Governmental Panel on Climate Change (IPCC) has confirmed that emissions resulting from human activities are significantly increasing the atmospheric concentration of the main greenhouse gases - carbon dioxide (CO_2), methane, and nitrogen oxides. This is likely to result in global warming.[29]

1.3.4 Carbon dioxide contributes about 70% of the direct effect due to these gases. Its relative contribution as the most important anthropogenic greenhouse gas will if anything increase into the next century.[30] The amount of CO_2 emitted is proportional to the quantity of carbon burnt in fuel usage, and fuel usage in the transport sector is closely linked with travel demand.

Transport, CO2 emissions and other pollutants

1.3.5 Transport is a major contributor to a range of greenhouse emissions and other pollutants. Table 2 indicates the relative contribution of transport to UK atmospheric emissions. The transport emissions relevant to global warming are as follows:

- **Carbon Dioxide (CO_2):** Road transport is directly responsible for about 20% of the UK's total man made CO_2 output. This is in the order of 0.6% of global CO_2 emissions;

- **Nitrogen Oxides (NOX):** Nearly half of UK emissions come from road vehicles. This proportion rises to 85% in urban areas;

- **Carbon Monoxide (CO):** The majority of CO emissions come from road vehicles. CO contributes to global warming indirectly through its contribution to surface ozone in photochemical smog and through oxiding to form CO_2; and

- **Volatile Organic Compounds (VOCs):** Road vehicles contribute 37% of VOCs. Sunlight acting on a mixture of VOCs and NOX produces ground level ozone and hence contributes to global warming.

1.3.6   A further indirect contribution to the greenhouse effect comes about through increased concentrations of ozone in the lower atmosphere caused by emissions of gases such as carbon monoxide (CO), nitrogen oxides (NOX) and volatile organic compounds (VOCs). The transport sector is a large contributor to these emissions. The halocarbons are also powerful greenhouse gases, though their global warming effect is offset by the decrease they cause to ozone concentrations in the upper atmosphere.

1.3.7 The UK transport sector has become an increasingly important generator of CO_2. As indicated in Figure 4, in 1979 transport was directly responsible for around 13% of total UK CO_2 emissions; by 1989 this proportion had risen to 20%, with 'indirect' transport emissions from refineries contributing an additional 3%. Between 1979-1989 transport was the only sector which experienced an absolute increase in CO_2 emission levels.[31]

1.3.8 Transport, and road transport in particular, is also a major source of pollutants, lead particulates and noise. It also involves a significant land take, can result in significant visual intrusion, and frequently creates severance. Reductions in travel demand will thus combat a major and growing contributor to UK greenhouse emissions, as well as bringing concomitant reductions in more local environmental problems.

Table 2 : The United Kingdom Atmospheric Emissions by Source: 1990

USE	Emission (Percentages)					
	Smoke	SO_2	NO_x	VOC[1]	CO	CO_2
Domestic	33	3	2	2	4	14
Commercial	1	2	2	-	-	5
Power Stations	6	72	28	-	1	34
Refineries	1	3	1	*	-	3
Agriculture	-	-	-	*	-	-
Other industry	13	16	8	2	4	23
Railways	-	-	1	-	-	-
Roads	46	2	51	41	90	19
Civil aviation[2]	-	-	1	-	-	-
Shipping[2]	1	2	5	1	-	1
Total[3]	100	100	100	100	100	100

Source: Department of the Environment, Digest of Environmental Statistics, No. 14 1991

Notes: (1) Remaining 54% of VOCs are emitted by processes and solvents, gas leakage and forests
(2) These statistics only cover estimates of the United Kingdom aircraft up to a height of 1,000 metres, and those for ships only cover the United Kingdom territorial water (ie. up to 20 km off the shore). So the figures will tend to understate the proportion of emissions from ships and aircraft.
(3) Figures may not add up to 100% due to rounding.

Table 3 : Changes in Road and Rail Travel (1979,1983,1989)

Mode	(billion vehicle kilometres).[1]					
	1979	%	1983	%	1989[2]	%
Cars and Taxis[3]	201.3	70.1	231.4	72.9	326.9	75.0
Motor Cycles	6.4	2.2	8.3	2.6	6.3	1.4
Larger Buses/Coaches[4]	3.3	1.1	3.6	1.1	4.4	1.0
Goods Vehicles	45.3	15.7	44.7	14.1	64.8	14.9
All Motor Vehicles	256.3	89.3	288.0	90.7	402.6	92.4
Rail	30.7	10.7	29.5	9.3	33.2	7.6
Total	287.0	100	317.5	100	435.8	100

Source: Department of Transport (1990), Transport Statistics, Great Britain.

Notes: (1) Traffic (vehicle kilometres) estimated are derived from the lengths of the road network in place each year
(2) Provisional estimates;
(3) Includes three wheeled cars, excludes all vans whether licensed for private or commercial use
(4) The bus and coach figures include the larger buses owned by non-PSV and foreign operators, but exclude all minibuses with 12 seats or less.

The contributors to transport emissions

1.3.9   The trends in the emissions from road vehicles in the period 1979 to 1989 are shown in Figure 5. The figure illustrates the close correspondence between the increase in vehicle kilometerage and the increase in CO_2 emissions.

1.3.10   Table 3 illustrates the contribution made to total kilometerage by different vehicles types in 1979, 1983 and 1989. Cars and taxis accounted for over 80% of the increase in motor vehicle kilometerage during this period. Thus, increases in travel demand have in large part been associated with the increased ownership and use of private cars.

1.3.11   This is particularly serious because, as illustrated in Table 4, road transport is the most polluting travel mode. For example, car CO_2 emissions per passenger kilometre are nearly twice as great as those for rail. For freight, emissions per tonne kilometre are over four times as great from road freight as from rail freight. However, such comparisons are highly sensitive to assumptions and behaviour concerning load factors for passenger transport and capacity utilisation in the case of freight.

Table 4 : **Emissions Generated Per Unit Travelled (1988)**

Mode	CO_2 Emissions/million passenger km (tonnes)
Passenger:	
Car	35.74
Rail	19.51
Freight:	
Road	220.0
Rail	50.0

Source: Transnet, (1990) Energy, Transport and the Environment.

1.3.12   The relationships between travel and energy consumption (and hence CO_2 emissions) for different modes and occupancy levels are illustrated in Table 5. The following key points can be made:

- As far as *mode* is concerned, railways and buses have the lowest energy consumption per passenger kilometre;

- *Load factors* can markedly influence energy consumption. A fully-laden small petrol car has a similar energy consumption per passenger kilometre to a half-laden inter-city train;

- Energy usage is dependent upon *vehicle efficiency* and engine capacity. There have, however, been marked improvements in the energy efficiency of cars and buses. During the period 1978 to 1988, CO_2 emissions fell by approximately 7% on a per vehicle kilometre basis. Reductions in other emissions were higher. Diesel engines are more fuel efficient than petrol engines;

- Energy usage is dependent on *trip characteristics*. Short journeys may be relatively inefficient whilst engines reach normal operating temperatures and CO_2 emissions decrease with improved traffic flows. Congestion, with its low average speeds and stop-go character, increases emissions for a given overall distance travelled. It has been estimated, for example, that 25% of all fuel used in urban areas is used by vehicles whilst they are stationary; and

- Fuel consumption also varies with *driving behaviour*. Speed is a particularly important factor. Driving at 110kph can use up to 30% more petrol than driving at 80kph.[32]

1.3.13   Clearly, a forward-looking study of this type needs to consider the robustness of such relationships. It is likely, for example, that there will continue to be steady increases in motor vehicle efficiencies, driven by a combination of legislative and market factors. However, the widespread introduction of catalytic convertors, which decrease vehicle efficiency and, therefore, marginally increase CO_2 emissions whilst removing other pollutants, may slow this trend.[33]

1.3.14   Economic growth may be associated with the use of bigger and more powerful cars. There appears little prospect, then, that private, partially-occupied motor vehicles will, in the short and medium-term future, radically improve their relative standing in terms of energy per passenger kilometre, without major policy changes.

Summary

1.3.15   The contribution of transport emissions to the environment can be summarised as follows:

- The International Panel on Climate Change has confirmed that global warming is occurring and has identified carbon dioxide as the single most important greenhouse gas (1.3.2 and 1.3.3);

Figure 4: **The Relative Contribution of the Transport Sector to Total UK Carbon Dioxide Emissions**

1979
Total Emissions: 181 million tonnes

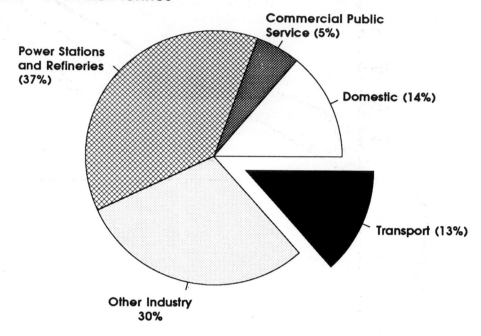

Power Stations and Refineries (37%)

Commercial Public Service (5%)

Domestic (14%)

Transport (13%)

Other Industry 30%

1989
Total Emissions: 157 million tonnes

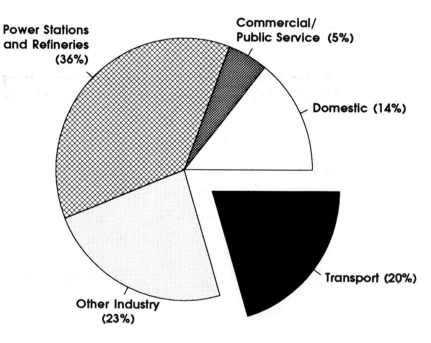

Power Stations and Refineries (36%)

Commercial/ Public Service (5%)

Domestic (14%)

Transport (20%)

Other Industry (23%)

Source: DoE Digest of Environmental Statistics

Figure 5: UK Trends in Emissions from Road Vehicles: 1979–1989

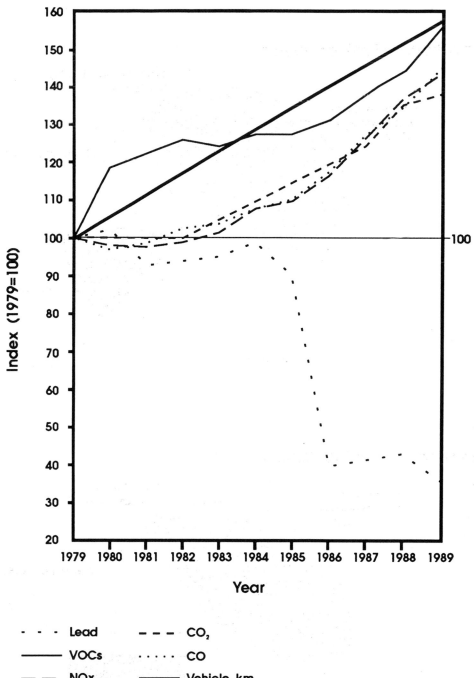

Source: DoE Digest of Environmental Statistics, 1990.

- Transport is a significant generator of carbon dioxide and is the only sector over the past decade which experienced a continued and significant increase in absolute emission levels (1.3.7);

- The relationship between travel demand and the level of emissions is complex because of the number of factors involved, including : mode, load factor, engine size, fuel type, trip distance, traffic flow and driving practices (1.3.12);

- The single most important explanation for the continued rise in CO_2 emissions from transport in the UK has been the increase in travel by the private motor car (1.3.10);

- Car use is particularly damaging in the urban environment since journeys are typically short and in congested conditions.[34] Both of these factors increase emissions for any given length of travel (1.3.12); and

Table 5 : **Energy Consumption for Different Passenger Transport Modes at Different Occupancy Rates**

Mode	(in MJ primary energy/passenger -km) Occupancy Rate			
	25%	50%	75%	100%
Gasoline Car				
< 1.4 litres	2.61	1.31	0.87	0.62
1.4 - 2.0 litres	2.98	1.49	0.99	0.75
> 2.0 litres	4.65	2.33	1.55	1.16
Diesel car				
< 1.4 litres	2.26	1.13	0.75	0.57
1.4 - 2.0 litres	2.76	1.38	0.92	0.69
> 2.0 litres	3.65	1.83	1.22	0.91
Railways				
Intercity	1.14	0.57	0.38	0.29
Super sprinter	1.31	0.66	0.44	0.33
Suburban electrical line	1.05	0.59	0.35	0.26
High-Speed train 300 km/h type:				
Brussels - Paris	2.86	1.43	0.96	0.72
High speed train 300 km/h type:				
London - Paris	2.50	1.25	0.83	0.62
Bus/car				
Double decker	0.70	0.35	0.23	0.17
Bus	1.17	0.58	0.39	0.29
Minibus	1.42	0.71	0.47	0.35
Express car	0.95	0.50	0.33	0.25
Air - Boeing 727	5.78	2.89	1.94	1.45
"Soft" transport - Cycling				0.06
Walking				0.16

Source: *Commission of the European Communities EC (1992), The Impact of Transport on the Environment. Com (92) 46.*

Notes: (1) Intercity in this context refers to standard commuter class urban rail systems

- Emissions of nitrogen oxide and sulphur dioxide from cars will be reduced by the fitting of catalytic converters to car exhausts. However, this will reduce vehicle energy efficiency and so marginally increase emissions of CO_2 (1.3.13).

1.3.16 In the short and medium-term future, it is unlikely that private, partially-occupied motor vehicles will improve their poor relative standing in terms of energy per passenger kilometre. Any contribution that the planning policies examined in this study could make to reducing travel demand or encouraging modal choice away from private motor vehicles would help reduce emissions that contribute to global warming and bring concomitant reductions in more local environmental problems.

c

1.4 Approaches to Reducing Transport Emissions and the Scope for a Planning Contribution

Introduction

1.4.1 The focus of this report is on land-use planning measures that might reduce travel demand and hence CO_2 and other pollutants from transport. Before reviewing the evidence to inform the scope for these measures, it is helpful to review briefly other possible approaches such as:

- technological measures to increase fuel efficiency and smooth traffic flows;

- influencing demand through economic measures, road management and regulation;

- influencing demand through the provision of infra-structure, for example public transport; and

- influencing demand through education.

In practice these responses are likely to be complementary and could be integrated with planning measures.

Technological measures

1.4.2 Possible technological measures include :

- improving engine and fuel efficiency and engine management systems;

- limiting the maximum power output of vehicles;

- improving vehicle maintenance; and

- limiting maximum speeds.

1.4.3 In the longer term, technological developments could also lead to the use of less-polluting fuels and power sources. Energy prices are likely to be a significant influence on the rate of development and diffusion of these measures. However, the current economic and legislative environment is not providing a strong impetus for these developments.

1.4.4 Thus, it is anticipated that there will be only slow increases in the energy efficiency of all modes and the rate of improvement is likely to be lower than the rate of increase in travel demand. Also, in so far as technological measures would not reduce travel demand, there could - if this were the only response - be wider detrimental environmental impacts. For example, the UK has a high level of vehicle owner-ship per kilometre of road. Increases in travel demand would be associated with increased congestion, unless additional road capacity were provided. There is a limit to the resource and wider environmental costs that could be sustained to meet such increases in demand particularly in urban areas. Nevertheless, it is important that the planning policies put forward in this report take account of the possibilities of technological measures.

Influencing demand through economic measures, road management and regulation

1.4.5 A number of economic measures have been identified as mechanisms for reducing travel demand and hence CO_2 emissions. These include carbon taxes, road pricing, vehicle pricing and taxation. In so far as these measures induce increases in the real costs of private motor travel, they are likely to lead to some reduction in travel demand and hence transport emissions. However, there is considerable debate over their effectiveness in this regard. Measures such as road pricing may be more relevant to the efficient allocation of road capacity, easing congestion and funding road infrastructure than to reducing overall travel demand. Vehicle pricing and taxation policies could encourage shifts to lower-powered cars, but effectively through taxing ownership rather than use. Road management and regulatory measures, such as the control of car parking, are also relevant as traffic demand management measures at the urban scale and may have significant impacts on modal choice. Certainly pricing policies to encourage the use of alternatives to the private motor car will be less effective if planning policies do not encourage development patterns that facilitate public transport use.

Influencing demand through the provision of non-car infrastructure

1.4.6 As indicated in Table 5, there are marked differences between the energy consumption and hence emissions-efficiency of different modes. The provision of public transport can be an important contributor to encouraging modal choice towards more energy-efficient means of travel. It may also, be a necessary concomitant of the planning measures proposed to reduce travel demand. Planning can also help create the circumstances in which more fuel-efficient alternative modes to the motor car (walking, cycling, public transport) become more attractive. Thus, it is important that the implementation of planning measures should be closely coordinated with the provision of infrastructure which encourages the use of other modes.

Influencing demand through education

1.4.7 Travel demand is influenced by the aspirations and motivations of individuals. The private motor car has assumed a status beyond its utility value as a means of transport. There is a lack of general acknowledgement or appreciation of the environmental disbenefits associated with increasing levels of car usage and fuel consumption. By contrast, the use of more emissions-efficient modes is often viewed unfavourably. If reductions in emissions from transport are to be achieved, significant changes in travel behaviour and attitudes towards emissions-efficient modes will be required. Planning can perhaps play a part in this, for example, through encouraging developments that demonstrate the possibilities for reducing travel demand.

Land-use planning and other measures

1.4.8 The implementation of planning policies to reduce travel demand will clearly need to:

- take account of technological developments;

- be applied so as to anticipate and complement economic measures, road management and regulations;

- be implemented in co-ordination with policies for the provision of infrastructure; and

- contribute through, for example, demonstration projects and educational initiatives to influence travel behaviour and improve attitudes towards emissions-efficient modes.

The scope for land-use planning

1.4.9 Before turning in the next part of the report to an analysis of the relationship between land-use planning factors and transport emissions, it is useful to review the scope for planning to reduce transport emissions.

1.4.10 As stressed above (1.2.14), the UK does not, in terms of international comparisons, exhibit the extremes of travel demand and per capita energy consumption for travel. This is probably a consequence of a relatively high overall population density and the concentration of the population within urban areas, which are themselves reasonably dense and which have urban structures that mainly predate the widespread use of the private motor car. The potential scope for reductions in transport emissions is therefore less than that evident in, for example, the US and Australia.[35] As noted, in general terms, towns and cities in the UK are similar in density and travel demand per capita to their counterparts in Continental Europe. The high overall population density of the UK, and the close juxtaposition of towns and cities, also limits the extent of self-containment that is likely to be achievable. Although there is clearly substantial scope for reduced energy consumption per head, it may be that the UK's overall potential for improvement is also less than that of some other more sparsely-populated European nations.

1.4.11 Most land uses change only slowly. Comprehensive and up-to-date information on these changes is only now becoming available. However, the following observations can be made:

- The annual rate of construction of industrial floorspace is less than 1% gross of the total stock. The amount of land involved may well be greater than this, as new industrial developments tend to be at a lower site density than the existing stock;

- The annual rate of construction of offices has been of the order of 2-3% gross of the existing stock. The space demands of users have become increasingly sophisticated and it is not unusual for twenty year-old buildings to be considered obsolete. An increasing proportion of all employment is in offices. Within the next twenty years both an expansion of the stock and substantial volumes of refurbishment will be subject to planning control;

- The annual rate of construction of retail floorspace is of the order of 1-2% gross of the stock, but amongst market leaders in the convenience food sector the rates of renewal tend to be considerably higher in the order of 8% per annum. Here, again, the planning system has the opportunity, over time, to strongly influence location patterns; and

- The number of new dwellings built each year represents around 1% - 1.5% gross of the total stock. Given the characteristics of the existing stock and the forecast increase in the numbers of households (particular additional single elderly person households), there will remain pressures for the allocation of additional housing land. Thus, there will be a substantial opportunity for the planning system to influence both locations and intensity. However, the rate of change that could be effected will be modest.

1.4.12 It is also necessary, when considering the possible contribution that planning can make, to take account of commitments in plans and permissions already granted. This will limit the scope for new policy directions to influence outcomes for some years to come.

1.4.13 One of the simulations undertaken in the study illustrated for a particular locality the order of magnitude of the change in emissions levels, relative to what would otherwise occur, that planning, complemented by public transport investment might make over a 20-year period. The results, described in

Appendix 1, suggested that each of three combined planning and transport investment options offer emissions reductions compared with a "do-minimum option". The simulation suggested that the option of extending public transport provision and regenerating existing centres whilst limiting the increase in highway capacity might provide a reduction in projected emissions in the order of 16%. These findings are similar to the results of other modelling work exploring the possible influence of land-use structure on energy use, and hence emissions, which indicate that as much as 10-15% savings in fuel use for passenger transport might be achieved through land-use changes at the city region scale over a 25-year period. [36]

1.4.14 Finally, as discussed above, travel demand has increased with economic growth and car ownership and through the extension of car usage. This may have been encouraged by trends in the real private costs of car transport and the opportunities afforded to travel further and more quickly and with great flexibility. There is some risk that any reductions in travel demand for a particular purpose which are achieved through planning could be offset by increases in travel for other purposes. Evidence, such as the similarities in time spent travelling by car and non-car owning households, would support such a contention.[37]

Summary

1.4.15 By way of summary the following points can be stressed:

- There are likely to be technological measures that will reduce CO_2 emissions from transport. However, these are unlikely to lead to marked reductions in emissions in the foreseeable future(1.4.4);

- There are a range of other policy measures that could reduce travel demand and emissions. The implementation of planning policies to reduce travel demand needs to be co-ordinated with such measures (1.4.8);

- The United Kingdom is a densely-populated, highly-urbanised country with an established urban structure. There is probably not the same scope for reductions in transport emissions through planning in the UK that appears evident in Australian and US cities (1.4.10);

- Most land uses change only slowly, but high travel-generating uses, such as offices, convenience retail, and leisure developments are renewed more rapidly, providing greater scope for planning to influence travel behaviour (1.4.11);

- One of the simulations undertaken in this study indicated that planning policies in combination with public transport measures could reduce projected transport emissions by 16% over a 20-year period. These findings are similar to those of other work which indicates that 10-15% savings in fuel usage for passenger transport might be achieved through land use changes at the city region scale over a 25-year period (1.4.13); and

- The scope for planning to reduce travel demand could be limited by tendencies for individuals and households to spend any time saved by reductions in travel for one purpose (such as journeys to work) on journeys for other purposes[38] (1.4.14).

Part II Inter-relationships Between Land Use, Transport Infrastructure and Travel Behaviour

2.1 Introduction: Land Use and Travel Demand Interaction

2.1.1 Part I above indicates that a wide variety of social and economic changes, together with technological developments, are continuing to widen the areas over which people and businesses conduct their activities. These trends have significant direct implications for travel demand. Many of these same changes are also contributing to the observed weakening of the traditional structure of urban areas, through reducing the centralisation of services, such as retailing, and permitting the wider dispersion and spatial separation of activities. It is the wider relationship between such land-use changes and both the increase in travel and the decline in the proportion of travel demand met by public transport, which provides the potential point of influence for the planning system. This topic forms the subject of this part of the report.

2.1.2 The interrelationships between land-use patterns and travel behaviour are too complex and insufficiently well understood to be comprehensively modelled in a form which would be useful in the current context. The spatial distribution of population and activity clearly has an important bearing on the need for, and potential benefits from, different types of travel. Equally, the patterns of accessibility associated with the available transport infrastructure and other determinants of real travel costs are an important influence on pressures for changes in the spatial distribution of land uses. As indicated in Part I, the approach to these issues has been a pragmatic one, drawing upon a wide variety of evidence including existing research studies, statistical analysis of available data, simulations, new survey work and broader case studies.

2.1.3 The material in this part of the report is organised as follows:

- Section 2.2 analyses the relationship between population density and travel behaviour;

- Section 2.3 considers the influence of the population size of urban areas and other types of settlement on travel demand;

- Section 2.4 explores the influence of a range of aspects of urban and regional structure on travel behaviour; and

- Section 2.5 reviews evidence on the impact of transport infrastructure on development pressures.

Further explanation of the statistical analyses undertaken in the study which inform this part of the report are given in Appendix 4 and the notes referenced in the text.

2.2 Population Density and Travel Demand

Introduction

2.2.1 The potential role of density in influencing both the distances people travel and their choice of mode has been explored in a variety of studies in the UK and elsewhere.[39] Some of the evidence from these studies is briefly reviewed below. Density can impact on travel behaviour in at least four ways:

(i) Higher population densities widen the range of opportunities for the development of local personal contacts and activities which can be maintained without resort to motorised transport;

(ii) Higher population densities within a specified locality increase the scale of local expenditure, widening the range of services which can potentially be supported and, in turn, reducing the need for travel to centres elsewhere;

(iii) Higher density patterns of development will tend to reduce average distances between place of residence and the places at which services, employment or other opportunities can be accessed. This potentially reduces the need for travel and increases the practicability of using non-motorised modes. This issue emphasises the potential relevance of both the density of population in urban areas as a whole as well as that of residential neighbourhoods, although the two effects are in practice difficult to distinguish; and

(iv) Within any given structure of urban area, increasing the density of population implies greater numbers of personal movements along specific corridors, improving the potential viability of public transport. Equally, higher densities may impose a range of constraints on the

ownership and use of private vehicles. Both of these factors have potential implications for modal choice.

Direct Evidence from the Study

2.2.2 Table 6 shows distance travelled in kilometres per week per person by mode and for all modes in 1985/6 in areas of different population density - defined in terms of persons per hectare - based upon a special analysis of National Travel Survey data. It shows that distance travelled by all modes and by car falls continuously with increasing density. Travel by other modes - with the exception of the "other" cate-

Table 6   Distance Travelled per Person per Week by Mode and Population Density: 1985/6

Density (Persons per hectare	All modes	Car	Local bus	Rail	Walk	Other[1]
			(kilometres)			
Under 1	206.3	159.3	5.2	8.9	4.0	28.8
1-4.99	190.5	146.7	7.7	9.1	4.9	21.9
5-14.99	176.2	131.7	8.6	12.3	5.3	18.2
15-29.99	152.6	105.4	9.6	10.2	6.6	20.6
30-49.99	143.2	100.4	9.9	10.8	6.4	15.5
50 and over	129.2	79.9	11.9	15.2	6.7	15.4
All Areas[2]	**159.6**	**113.8**	**9.3**	**11.3**	**5.9**	**19.1**

Source: National Travel Survey, 1986

Notes: (1) Other refers to two-wheeled motor vehicles, taxis, domestic air travel, other public transport and other types of bus (school, hire, express and works).

(2) Data exclude all trips less than 1.6km and only refer to the main mode used for a trip. It therefore excludes the walking element of all non walk trips.

(3) Population density figures were taken from the OPCS sampling frame which is based on the Postcode Address File. Population Figures were from the 1981 Census.

gory - tends to rise with density. However, with the exception of bus travel, the relationships are not entirely smooth.

2.2.3 Table 7, from the same source, shows the average number of journeys per week made by persons residing in areas of different density by mode and for all modes. The number of journeys are clearly non-linearly related to population density, first rising and then falling as density increases. By contrast, the numbers of journeys by bus and walk rise continuously with density.

***Table 7* Number of Journeys per Person per Week by Mode and Population Density: 1985/86**

Density (Persons per hectare	All modes	(kilometres) Car	Local bus	Rail	Walk	Other[1]
Under 1	13.59	9.72	0.55	0.11	1.40	1.81
1-4.99	14.81	10.28	1.04	0.23	1.78	1.48
5-14.99	14.69	10.10	1.28	0.25	1.87	1.19
15-29.99	14.12	8.74	1.53	0.24	2.38	1.24
30-49.99	13.97	8.38	1.77	0.37	2.33	1.12
50 and over	12.99	6.68	2.21	0.63	2.47	1.00
All Areas[2]	**13.98**	**8.75**	**1.52**	**0.33**	**2.14**	**1.25**

Source: National Travel Survey, 1986

Notes: (1) Other refers to two-wheeled motor vehicles, taxis, domestic air travel, other public transport and other types of bus (school, hire, express and works).

(2) Data exclude all trips less than 1.6km and only refer to the main mode used for a trip. It therefore excludes the walking element of all non walk trips.

(3) Population density figures were taken from the OPCS sampling frame which is based on the Postcode Address File. Population Figures were from the 1981 Census.

2.2.4 Density also emerges as a significant explanatory variable in a number of the statistical analyses which were undertaken. The conclusions relevant at the standard planning region and urban case study district levels are given below.

Standard Planning Region

2.2.5 In the analysis at standard planning region level, density emerged as having a positive influence on the proportion of work-related travel undertaken by public transport, although any impact on reducing distance travelled appears marginal. There is also some indication of a weakening over time of the relationship between density and use of public transport. There is some suggestion in the data that higher density tends to reduce non-work travel and to increase the proportion of non-work travel which is undertaken by walking.[40/41] However, the interpretation of the evidence at this level is complicated by the

difficulties in distinguishing the general effects of density from those of urbanisation.

Urban Case Study Areas

2.2.6 Whilst the effects of population density and the proportion of an area which is urbanised are again difficult to separate statistically, population density emerges as an important explanation of the travel characteristics of the areas considered in the majority of the analyses (although interestingly not in the analysis of the proportion using car for travel to work). The evidence suggests that:

- higher density reduces average distance travelled to work;[42]
- higher density reduces the total amount of car travel in the district;[43] and
- higher densities increase the proportion of travel to work which is undertaken by public transport.[44]

Indirect Evidence from the Study

2.2.7 A variety of other evidence from the study is also relevant in the context of exploring the travel implications of possible changes in residential densities.

Simulations of Alternative Development Patterns

2.2.8 The evidence here is drawn from simulations for two of the case study areas - described in more detail in Appendix 1. These simulations assessed the implications for distance travelled and, in one area, modal split of alternative locations for given levels of housing and employment development. The results indicate that the urban infill options involve somewhat lower distances travelled and less fuel consumption. However, their advantages in terms of distance travelled, compared with the worst options considered, were less than 3% in one case and less than 1% in the other. The urban infill approach also performed better in terms of modal split than the low-density peripheral expansion option, although the difference was less than 0.2%, and it performed less well in these terms than the linear expansion option.

2.2.9 It is important to recognise that these results, which to a substantial extent reflect the current travel behaviour of residents of different types of area, will also be influenced by issues of structure - which is considered below - as well as by density.

Neighbourhood Survey Evidence

2.2.10 There appears to be no clear overall relationship in the data collected between the population density of neighbourhoods and the proportion of trips which are made by private car. However, possibly more valid comparisons - given the wide range of variables influencing travel demand - can be made by examining neighbourhoods with contrasting densities within the same urban area. Analysing the data in this way indicates the following points:

- Neighbourhoods with higher densities tend to have a larger proportion of shorter-distance trips to frequently-used local facilities, a greater proportion of which are undertaken on foot. This is mirrored in a smaller proportion of total trips being undertaken by car than in the lower-density neighbourhoods within the same urban area;

- This relationship holds even across neighbourhoods where car-ownership rates and occupational characteristics are similar; and

- In one case study area, where the relationship does not appear to hold, car-ownership rates are much higher in the high-density neighbourhood. Car usage in this neighbourhood is, however, only slightly higher than in the relatively lower-density neighbourhood. Nevertheless, the proportion of shorter-distance trips and the proportion of walk journeys remains higher than those in the lower-density neighbourhood.

This analysis suggests that density is not merely acting as a "proxy" for income, but it is an important explanatory variable capable of influencing travel behaviour in its own right.

2.2.11 A number of other findings of the neighbourhood survey work are also relevant in this context.

- The range and quality of facilities offered by local centres, especially the availability of food shops, is an important determinant of the extent to which people use neighbourhood centres, rather than travel to centres elsewhere. The facilities which an area can support will, in turn, partly be determined by the population density of an area. The availability of facilities turns out to be substantially more important in the survey findings than transport-related factors-such as the availability of public transport and parking at local centres - in determining the use made of neighbourhood facilities. However, the usage of local facilities is also related to the proportion of an area's population which is retired, unemployed or at home for other reasons. The scope for higher residential densities to influence the use made of local facilities may, therefore, vary across different population groups;

- The frequency with which people use their local centres is closely related to the distance to the centre, and to the relative distance from their home of the local and non-local centres. For example, the average distance to local centres which individuals use on a daily basis is 1.3 km, compared to 3.4 km for those which are used on a monthly basis. Again, as argued above, there are clear reasons for believing that the average distance to local centres and density are related; and

- There is also a clear relationship in the survey results between distance to local centres and mode of travel. For example, whereas walking accounts for 53% of trips of up to 1.6 km, it accounts for only 12% of trips in the range of 1.6 - 4.8 km. For the latter trips, car and bus account for 44% and 43% of trips respectively.

Evidence from Other Studies

2.2.12 The role of density has been highlighted in a range of UK studies including, for example, work by the Transport and Road Research Laboratory (TRRL) and Hillman and Whalley. [45] At the international level the major work on the influence of density is that of Newman and Kenworthy who, in a study of petrol consumption in a range of major cities across the world, show that energy consumption falls as density rises (Figure 6). [46] The evidence at the international level that density is a significant determinant of travel behaviour is a useful wider confirmation of its potential significance in the UK.

2.2.13 The major European cities considered by Newman and Kenworthy appear to be fairly similar in terms of both petrol consumption and density. Along with the clear evidence that the rate at which petrol consumption falls decreases as density increases, this might suggest that the scope in the UK for increases in urban density to reduce car travel may be limited. However, it must be recognised that a substantial, and growing, proportion of the UK's population lives outside of major cities and at densities much lower than those of the European cities included in Figure 6.

Inter-Related Issues

2.2.14 Whilst the evidence reviewed above supports the view that density plays a significant role in influencing travel behaviour, the interpretation of this evidence and the derivation of conclusions in relation to possible future planning policies needs to take account of several complicating factors.

Density, Location and Income Levels

2.2.15 Within the UK the highest residential densities are predominantly found in areas close to urban centres, reflecting historic patterns of urbanisation and subsequent suburbanisation. The proximity of these high-density neighbourhoods to central area services and employment opportunities raises questions about the extent to which the differences in travel behaviour in higher density areas can be wholly attributed to the effects of density.

Figure 6 **Gasoline Use per Capita versus Population Density (1980)**

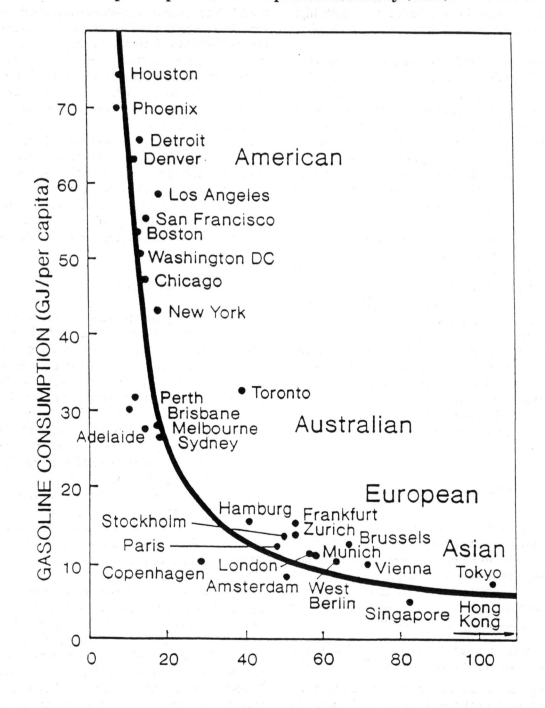

Source: Newman, P and Kenworthy, J., Cities and Automobile Dependence, Gower: Aldershot, 1989.

2.2.16 More importantly, in Britain, there is a strong negative relationship between the population density of residential areas and the average income levels of their residents. Lower income levels in high-density areas will have implications for both lifestyles and levels of car ownership. This again warns against drawing simple conclusions about the independent effects of density and, in particular, on the extent to which a policy of favouring higher density in new suburban developments will have beneficial effects on travel behaviour. It should also be noted that car-ownership is a poor proxy for income levels in both high and low-density areas.

2.2.17 In principle, the effects of density, location and income levels could be separated by a statistical analysis which controls for the latter two variables. However, the necessary data for this analysis are not available. Some of the data which are available suggest that socio-economic factors - and in particular car ownership - are more significant than density per se in explaining inter-personal and inter-area variations in travel behaviour. However, it would be wrong to read too much into this result.

2.2.18 The analysis of the dataset shown in Table 6 above is not entirely conclusive because of the combination of the limited number of observations, and the fact that some relationships are clearly non-linear. However, the work did not suggest that differences in travel behaviour between areas could simply be explained by variations in car ownership. Density still emerges as a significant variable in many of the statistical analyses where car ownership variables are included. The wide range of studies which have identified density as an important explanatory factor in travel behaviour in very different contexts also supports the view that it exerts an independent effect on travel.

Congestion Effects

2.2.19 In a number of the traffic model simulations which were undertaken for the case study areas, the potential benefits, in terms of energy consumption, from focusing development at high density in inner urban areas, rather than at lower density in more peripheral locations, were reduced or outweighed by two types of congestion-related effect:

- the reduction in vehicle-operating efficiencies associated with more congested conditions; and

- re-routing - and hence increases in distances travelled - by some vehicles seeking to avoid congested central area conditions. In one case these caused a more dispersed pattern of infill to perform better in energy consumption terms than the most concentrated development option.

2.2.20 The short-term impact of congestion in mitigating the potential transport benefits of higher-density development may be overstated over the daytime period as a whole by the use of models which are designed to replicate peak-period conditions. However, it needs to be borne in mind in this context that the recent integrated transport strategy studies undertaken in many metropolitan areas suggest that future off-peak travel conditions will increasingly become like those of the present peak.[47]

2.2.21 The effect of congestion also needs to be taken into account in assessing the total potential environmental benefits of higher-density development. In a number of the case study areas existing levels of congestion are thought to have severe environmental disbenefits. The congestion issues which arise where options for high-density development in inner urban locations are considered will, however, be less relevant to the assessment of the potential costs and benefits of increasing the density of development in suburban and other non-central locations. More generally, the complications posed by congestion point to the need for complementary policies to favour the use of public transport if a policy in favour of higher-density residential developments is to be pursued.

Adaptive Behaviour

2.2.22 Encouraging an increase in residential densities may conflict with residential preferences. Historically, people have used the opportunities presented by new transport infrastructure to seek out new, lower-density residential locations. The strong inverse relationship between density and income also points to a preference for a high level of personal space. The risks are, therefore, that both the welfare costs of the policy may be significant and that its effects could be to some extent frustrated by adaptive behaviour within the housing market. For example, higher-income groups may respond to constraints on the supply of new, low-density property by focusing their search for housing to a greater extent on the existing stock, perhaps increasing decentralisation to other suburban and rural locations.

2.2.23 The risk of this type of adaptive response to planning controls arises in relation to a number of approaches considered within the study. Its likely influence is difficult to judge since the effect cannot be modelled in a satisfactory way and there is no good relevant case study evidence. As discussed in Appendix 2, the effects of the policy may therefore depend on the success of other urban policies aimed at improving the quality of the urban environment. Measures to facilitate the maintenance and improvement of older housing, its conversion to smaller units and the conversion of unoccupied spaces in commercial buildings for residential uses, may be able to maintain or increase densities without resorting to town cramming. Better public transport and mass transit systems and attractive opportunities for walking and cycling should have mutually-beneficial effects on travel demand. Evidence on how to enhance the perceived attractiveness of higher-density living, including demonstration projects, may also have a useful complementary role in minimising adverse, adaptive responses, as discussed in Part IV.

Summary

2.2.24 The balance of evidence presented in this section supports the view that higher densities in residential development would both reduce travel and increase the proportion of travel demand met by modes other than car(2.2.2-2.2.13). Determining precisely where key thresholds are is problematic given the level of disaggregation of available data. Travel demand rises quickly as density falls below 15 persons per hectare and falls sharply as density increases above 50 persons per hectare (2.2.2.). However, in view of the fact that factors such as location and income are related to density (2.2.15 and 2.2.16), and because of the potential for adaptive responses to changes in the densities of new development (2.2.22 and 2.2.23), it is likely that the net effects on travel behaviour - although positive -would be substantially less than would be indicated by simplistic comparisons of existing travel behaviour in areas of different density (2.2.16).

2.2.25 Furthermore, the potential benefits, in terms of energy consumption from focusing development at high density in urban areas may be reduced by lower vehicle-operating efficiencies associated with more congested conditions and increases in distance travelled due to rerouting (2.2.19).

2.2.26 Complementary planning policies will thus be required to ensure increased residential densities do not result in a deterioration in the quality of urban life (2.2.23). This, in turn, will reduce the risks associated with potential adaptive responses from high-income groups and maximise the beneficial effects on travel demand arising from higher densities.

2.3 Population Size and Travel Demand

Introduction

2.3.1 Debates on strategic planning issues in Britain in recent years have tended to be dominated by questions relating to the allocation of new housing development. The relationship between the size of areas, in population terms, and their travel characteristics is an issue of some importance in the context of decisions about the expansion of different types of settlements or, in appropriate cases, the creation of new settlements.

2.3.2 The assumption is that as an area becomes larger in population terms its capacity to support a wider range of job opportunities and services will tend to increase, generating greater potential for self-containment. Larger areas may also be better able to support a wider range of public transport services, both to accommodate internal movements and travel to other centres. Conversely, with a given urban structure, the average distance between places of residence - from which 80-90% of trips arise or terminate - and opportunities for other activities will tend to increase as population increases. These conflicting considerations suggest, as turns out to be the case, that the relationship between population size and travel is unlikely to be a straightforward one.

Evidence From The Study

2.3.3 Table 8 sets out data from a special analysis of the 1986 National Travel Survey, showing how distance travelled for both work and non-work purposes varies with the population size of an area. In the case of the metropolitan areas the data relate to the specific areas; in the other cases - within which rural is

taken to cover settlements of less than 3,000 population - the data relate to all settlements falling within the relevant size band.

2.3.4 It is clear that there is no simple relationship between urban size and travel demand. Work travel is particularly high in Outer London. Whilst much lower in major urban areas, it starts to rise sharply as the population size of an area falls below 50,000. Non-work travel follows a roughly similar pattern, although in this case the population threshold below which distance travelled begins to rise sharply appears to be lower - around 25,000.

2.3.5 Whilst the issues in relation to the loss of population from London are not clear, the general implications of these data are that the decentralisation of population from the conurbations, and the more general relocation of people to smaller settlements seen in recent decades, is likely to have resulted in a substantial growth in travel demand. This is reflected in the rapid rise in the lengths of journeys to work in Central London from 9.5km in 1962 to 23km in 1985/86.

2.3.6 The analysis of travel-to-work census data certainly appears to support this contention. Over the period 1971 to 1981 there was a marked increase in trip lengths by train and car to workplaces. Whilst the effects on travel of population decentralisation raise important issues from a policy perspective, the data leave it unclear whether the different experience of Greater London reflects its relatively high income levels or a more fundamental tendency for travel to begin to increase with increasing urban size beyond some point. Equally, the data for the metropolitan counties raise questions about whether there is some 'U'-shaped relationship within the population range covered by these counties, or whether this reflects the economic conditions of Merseyside and Glasgow.

D

Table 8: Distance Travelled by Settlement Population Size: 1985/6

Area	Work Travel (kilometres per person per week)[1]		Non-Work Travel		Total	
	kms	(%)	kms	(%)	kms	(%)
Inner London	45.3	32.1	96.0	67.9	141.3	100.0
Outer London	58.3	35.0	108.3	65.0	166.6	100.0
West Midland urban area	37.5	30.9	83.7	69.0	121.2	100.0
Greater Manchester urban area	47.1	36.6	81.6	63.4	128.8	100.0
West Yorshire urban area	33.1	24.2	103.3	75.7	136.4	100.0
Glasgow urban area	28.6	31.4	62.5	68.6	91.2	100.0
Liverpool urban area	20.1	22.5	69.2	77.5	89.3	100.0
Tyneside urban area	28.9	26.4	80.4	73.6	109.3	100.0
Other urban areas over 250,000	37.1	26.3	104.0	73.7	141.2	100.0
Urban areas population 100,000 to 250,000	48.9	30.5	111.6	69.5	160.5	100.0
Urban areas population 50,000 to 100,000	45.4	29.4	109.0	70.6	154.5	100.0
Urban areas population 25,000 to 50,000	50.1	33.2	100.9	66.8	151.0	100.0
Urban areas population 3,000 to 25,000	51.7	29.4	123.9	70.6	175.7	100.0
Rural areas	65.9	31.2	145.2	68.8	211.0	100.0
All Areas	**48.5**	**30.3**	**111.1**	**69.6**	**159.6**	**100.0**

Source: National Travel Survey Data, 1986
Notes: (1) This excludes trips less 1.6km

2.3.7 Using the same areas, Table 9 shows the total absolute amount and proportions of travel which were undertaken by each mode in 1985/86 in the same areas. The data show a similar lack of a clear relationship between population size, car usage, and public transport usage within metropolitan areas. Elsewhere there is a tendency for the use of the car to rise as settlement size falls.

2.3.8 The balance of public transport usage between bus and rail varies greatly between metropolitan and non-metropolitan areas, with bus less important outside the metropolitan areas. Walking shows no clear relationship with population size, although it is particularly low in the smallest settlements. The decentralisation of population from both London and the metropolitan counties is likely to have been associated with a shift from public transport to car. Judged in terms of its impact on CO_2 emissions, this effect is likely to have been less significant than the increase associated with the overall growth in travel.

2.3.9 The extent to which the relationship between settlement size and travel is shaped by other factors has also been explored through the statistical analysis. This incorporates data on car ownership, the only relevant variable available for the whole set of areas defined in Table 8. The statistical relationships indicate that the use of public transport for travel to work increases with urban size. This may also have some effect in increasing the use of public transport for non-work purposes. In overall terms, the analysis suggests that increasing urban size tends to produce higher levels of travel, although this would probably change if Greater London was excluded. Greater urban size also reduces the proportion of work-related travel undertaken by car. Other than a possible effect on the proportion of non-work travel undertaken by public transport, there is no apparent simple overall statistical relationship in the 1986 data between urban size and non-work travel. (Interestingly though, a significant negative relationship between population size and non-work travel is evident in the earlier 1979 data.)

2.3.10 By contrast, car ownership has strong and, in all but two cases, significant effects in the expected direction of the statistical relationships.[48] It must be recognised, of course, that simple statistical models may be unable to capture the indirect effects through which urban size may influence travel via its impact on car ownership. For example, the greater availability of bus services and constraints on parking, and other limitations on private cars in inner city areas, may well act to depress ownership rates.

Table 9 **Total Distance Travelled by Mode and Settlement Population Size: 1985/86**

	(kilometres per person per week)[1]					
Area	All Modes	Car	Local Bus	Rail	Walking	Other[2]
	km	km %	km %	km %	km %	km %
Inner London	141.3	76.2 (54.0)	12.0 (8.5)	34.1 (24.1)	2.5 (1.8)	16.6 (11.6)
Outer London	166.6	113.3 (68.0)	8.9 (5.3)	23.3 (14.0)	2.6 (1.6)	18.5 (11.1)
West Midland urban area	121.2	83.8 (69.2)	14.8 (12.2)	5.5 (4.5)	3.2 (2.6)	13.9 (11.5)
Greater Manchester urban area	128.8	87.2 (67.7)	15.7 (12.2)	5.4 (4.2)	3.7 (2.8)	16.8 (13.1)
West Yorkshire urban area	136.4	85.5 (62.7)	17.7 (13.0)	3.2 (2.3)	3.6 (2.7)	26.4 (19.3)
Glasgow urban area	91.2	49.5 (54.3)	16.4 (18.0)	4.9 (5.3)	4.4 (4.9)	16.0 (17.5)
Liverpool urban area	89.3	54.0 (60.4)	17.1 (19.1)	6.1 (6.8)	2.6 (3.0)	9.5 (10.7)
Tyneside urban area	109.3	63.7 (58.2)	19.8 (18.1)	2.9 (2.7)	2.7 (2.5)	20.2 (18.5)
Other Urban areas over 250,000	141.2	93.6 (66.3)	11.2 (7.9)	8.3 (5.9)	4.2 (3.0)	23.9 (15.9)
Urban areas population 100,000 to 250,000	160.5	114.8 (71.5)	8.6 (5.4)	11.3 (7.0)	3.2 (2.0)	22.6 (14.1)
Urban areas population 50,000 to 100,000	154.5	110.4 (71.5)	7.2 (4.7)	13.0 (8.4)	3.7 (2.4)	20.2 (13.0)
Urban areas population 25,000 to 50,000	151.0	110.8 (73.4)	5.7 (3.8)	12.5 (8.3)	3.7 (2.5)	18.2 (12.1)
Urban areas population 3,000 to 25,000	175.7	133.4 (75.9)	7.2 (4.1)	8.0 (4.6)	3.0 (1.7)	24.1 (13.7)
Rural areas	211.0	163.8 (77.6)	5.7 (2.7)	10.9 (5.2)	1.7 (0.8)	28.9 (13.7)
All Areas	**159.6**	**113.8 (71.3)**	**9.3 (5.8)**	**11.3 (7.1)**	**3.2 (2.0)**	**22.0 (13.8)**

Source: National Survey Data, 1986
Notes: (1) Excludes trips under 1.6kms.
(2) Other refers to two wheeled motor vehicles, taxis, domestic air travel, other public transport and other types of bus.

2.3.11 Population size does not emerge as a significant factor in explaining any of the differences in travel behaviour between the urban case study areas in the statistical analyses. However, any relationship may be masked by the association within the case study areas between population size and density.[49]

• The decentralisation of population from urban areas to smaller rural settlements is associated with significant growth in travel;[53] and

• the largest new towns have tended to achieve the highest levels of self containment.[54]

Wider Evidence

2.3.12 The conclusions above are broadly consistent with the results from other relevant UK studies:

• Distance travelled by car decreases continuously with increasing urban size, with the notable exception of London - whereas distance travelled by public transport rises continuously with increasing urban size - even including the case of London.[50] The conclusion that distance travelled by car decreases with increasing urban size is also confirmed in other subsequent work;[51]

• Smaller remote settlements are particularly inefficient in transport energy terms. The most energy-efficient urban form is the larger town with a range of services, employment and public transport;[52]

Summary

2.3.13 There is no simple relationship between urban size and transport emissions. Work travel is particularly high in Outer London. Whilst much lower in major urban areas, it starts to rise sharply as the population size of an area falls below 50,000. Non-work travel follows a roughly similar pattern (2.3.4).

2.3.14 It is apparent from National Travel Survey data and statistical analyses that the process of dispersal of population from the major urban areas to smaller more rural settlements has probably added substantially to travel demand. It has also shifted the balance of demand from public transport to the private car in the process (2.3.9).

2.3.15 Small village developments and new settlement proposals of below 3,000 population are unlikely to be large enough to sustain the range of employment opportunities and social facilities required to achieve a reasonable degree of self containment. Previous work suggests that, where decentralisation does take place, an effort should be made to locate development in and around settlements with a population of at least 25,000 (preferably over 50,000) with a balance between employment opportunities and the economically-active population.

2.3.16 The issue of whether travel demand, and perhaps aspects of car usage, begin to rise again as the population size of areas reaches some point is less clear cut. A substantial part of the differences in travel behaviour between the major conurbations appears to be accounted for by differences in car ownership - and probably a range of associated income and life style factors (2.3.5). However, population size may also have complex impacts via its influence on car ownership.

LEEDS METROPOLITAN UNIVERSITY LIBRARY

2.4 The Influence of Urban and Regional Structures on Travel Demand

Introduction

2.4.1 This section of the report draws together evidence on the role of urban and regional structure in influencing travel. It considers:

- the issues of overall urban structure, focusing in particular on the effects of centralisation and other aspects of the location of travel-generating activities;

- the effects of a range of other urban characteristics on travel behaviour, focusing particularly on neighbourhood level issues; and

- the effects of a range of wider aspects of regional structure on travel demand.

Urban Structure

2.4.2. A range of conflicting issues are involved in questions about the travel implications of centralised versus alternative urban structures. The concentration of trip ends entailed in more centralised patterns of activity increases opportunities for multi-purpose trips, potentially reducing total travel. More importantly, it increases the viability and availability of public transport through focusing demand on radial corridors. The congestion and parking constraints associated with centralisation, also raise the costs and difficulties of private car use, with implications for modal choice.

2.4.3 Land-use patterns involving decentralised concentrations of activities have the potential to be more efficient in terms of the distance which people need to travel for particular types of facility. However, if people elect on a substantial scale not to utilise their nearest centres, this potential may not be realised, and the outcome may involve higher travel demand than overall centralisation. This may arise if the roles of individual centres within a polynuclear structure become significantly differentiated. This can be counteracted, to some extent, by ensuring that local centres have a range of services and facilities, as discussed below (2.4.23).

2.4.4. Similar issues arise in relation to the potential benefits from the intermixing of land uses. In principle this reduces average distances between place of residence and opportunities for employment and access to services. However, choice or specialisation within the labour market, or in the nature of services which are sought, may mean that people do not make use of the nearest local opportunities. In this case the effect of intermixing may be to create diffuse patterns of trips which cannot be served effectively by public transport.

Statistical Analyses : Effects of Centralisation

2.4.5 These issues were explored in the statistical analyses based upon NTS data. Because of the limitations on what data are available at the regional level, and the problem of defining and securing data for central areas in some of the case study districts, the proportion of total employment in largely office-based service activities was used as a proxy for centralisation.[55] On this basis centralisation emerged as having a powerful effect in favouring the use of public transport rather than car. In a purely statistical sense it also appears that centralisation is associated with longer average journeys to work. Other factors, such as the higher earnings and the more specialised nature of much central area office employment, rather than centralisation per se, may of course influence, or be responsible for, this latter finding.

2.4.6 The specific, key findings are that:

- at the regional level centralisation appears to have some effect of increasing average journey lengths. Centralisation also has strong effects of increasing the use of public transport and reducing the use of the car for travel to work;[56]

- at the regional level, centralisation has clear effects of increasing the use of public transport rather than the car for non-work travel;[57] and

- in the analyses of the data for the urban case study areas, centralisation has the clear effect of increasing journey lengths to work, and has similar effects on modal choice to those observed in the regional level analysis.

Case Study and Other Evidence in Relation to Employment Centralisation

2.4.7 The simulations pointed to advantages in terms of travel behaviour associated with options in which employment growth is located in or near to central areas. However, it is impossible to separate the effects of centralisation and population density in these simulations. Data which have been secured for a number of major office developments in the West Midlands (in city centre, suburban centre and peripheral locations), strongly support the conclusion that a higher proportion of travel to work to central areas is undertaken by public transport. Suburban centre locations show a lower use of public transport, whilst peripheral locations are particularly car dependent. The figures are summarised in Table 10.

2.4.8 The same data also indicate that, within city and suburban central area locations, proximity to a rail station is an important influence on modal choice. The proportion of journeys undertaken by train falls

from 11% for one office complex adjacent to a rail station, to 3% for a comparable development 200m away, to 0.4% for a development 500 metres away.

2.4.9 This data, and evidence from other case study areas, indicate that both occupational factors and the availability of private off-street parking are significant influences on modal choice within central area offices, although the data do not allow the separate influences of these factors to be considered simultaneously in any detail. However, data provided by the local authority for another of the case study areas indicate a strong association between the proportion of employees with a parking space available at their office and the proportion actually using cars for travel to work.[58] Other evidence from the case study areas also supports the view that the availability of parking at places of work is a crucial influence on modal choice in central areas.

2.4.10 Another study of 1981 Census travel-to-work data for 27 British towns and cities has confirmed the importance of centralisation on mode of journey to work.[59] Centralisation of employment is associated with relatively heavy use of public transport in general and of rail in particular. In every case considered, the reliance of an area upon public transport declines with increasing distance from the centre. However, city centre locations tend to involve journeys to work of above average length. Significantly, however, and in conflict with the analyses reported above, this study found that central locations, with the exception of London, do not appear to be associated with below average proportions of car trips. Rather, the higher modal share of public transport appeared to be primarily associated with less reliance on modes such as walking and cycling.

2.4.11 The role of centralisation of employment, in particular, in influencing modal choice also emerges in other studies. For example, J Michael Thompson's study of 30 international cities identifies the extent of centralisation of employment and facilities as a key determinant of modal choice, arguing that the physical problems of transporting large numbers of people

Table 10: **Mode of Travel to Work: Selected West Midlands Developments**

	Proportion of all Journeys to Work (%)					
	Central Birmingham		**Solihull Centre**		**Coventry Business Parks**	
Mode	Development 1	Development 2	Development 1	Development 2	Development 1	Development 2
Car Driver	33	45	72	66	76	79
Passenger	9	10	5	9	9	11
Bus	30	29	9	8	9	3
Train	28	16	11	3	1	0
Other	0	0	3	14	4	7

Source: West Midlands Joint Data Team & Centro, Selected Travel-to-Work Surveys, 1989-1992.

into concentrated centres govern the reliance on public transport.[60]

Polycentric Structures

2.4.12 It is difficult to make meaningful comparisons between the practical consequences of polycentric, as opposed to single-centre structures. There are issues of definition here since an urban structure such as Birmingham's - with its strong centre and hierarchy of district and local centres - is in some senses polycentric. However, the sub-centres in this case typically have only a limited role in employment terms. Much of their role lies in providing goods and services where local availability is an important consideration to users.

2.4.13 The analyses undertaken in the study did not identify major advantages in transport emissions from a polycentric structure consisting of several urban centres without a distinct hierarchy:

- the case study districts which form part of overall polycentric urban structures do not appear to have travel behaviour which is systematically different from that which would be expected based on their other characteristics; and

- simulations of alternative urban regeneration strategies for a major sub-region - described in Appendix 1 - in which a new district centre is created, performed less well on the relevant criteria than a strategy in which commercial investment is focused on existing centres.

Intermixing of Employment and Residential Land Uses

2.4.14 Whilst the physical separation of activities is a major determinant of travel demand, within urban areas the evidence suggests that the key factor involved is population density rather than the intermixing of land uses.[61] Two other sources of evidence suggest that - under conditions of current travel costs, with the growing emphasis on choice in personal behaviour and specialisation within the labour market - the intermixing of land uses is of limited importance as an influence on travel:

- The study simulations using strategic transport models suggest that intermixing residential and employment uses within a particular urban zone makes a negligible difference to distance travelled or modal choice compared to alternatives in which similar levels of growth take place in broadly the same part of the urban areas. It needs, however, to be borne in mind that such simulations cannot

consider the possibility of transfer to non-motorised modes. Nevertheless, the general insensitivity of travel behaviour to the physical relationship between land uses within urban areas has also been found in other modelling work. For example, a study of the Stockholm region using the TRAMA model, which tested the effects of six alternative patterns of location for the anticipated growth of houses and jobs over a thirty-year period, found a range of only 5% in the public/private travel split across the options considered;[62]

- Intermixing of land uses did not figure as an apparent explanation of differences in travel behaviour between the case study areas. Within these areas, the decline of manufacturing and the role of walking and cycling to work, means that intermixing has declined. The extent of the decline in intermixing is difficult to measure formally; and

- Empirical studies have indicated that decentralising workplaces to residential areas in the suburbs does not automatically lead to any corresponding reduction in either the number or length of work trips. The tendency is for people to select employment from the whole urban area and beyond with little regard for its nearness to home.[63] The converse is also true, with accessibility to employment being of minor significance in residential location decisions. This is reflected in the base travel matrices of the available transport models, which helps account for the relative insensitivity of travel patterns in the simulations to intermixing and other land-use options.

2.4.15 There will no doubt be circumstances at the local level in which intermixing may contribute to a reduction in travel demand, particularly through the decentralisation of less specialised forms of employment which generates demands that can be met from local labour markets. On balance, however, the evidence suggests that any consideration of policy options involving a more general intermixing of land uses has to rest largely on the future potential to reduce the need for car journeys rather than on the likely short-term impact on travel demand.

Location of Activities

Retail:

2.4.16 Simulation tests were carried out on the implications of locating a major retail development in alternative locations such as: a central area; a suburban and/or peripheral district; and, around an orbital bypass. Simulations were carried out in two case study areas. Both sets of simulations suggest that when trips associated with the particular development alone are considered, the central areas perform best in terms of vehicle kilometerage and energy consumption. In the simulation where it was considered, the orbital bypass location performed worst on these criteria, with other options falling in the middle of the range. However, the differences were not great: average journey lengths ranged from 10.6km to 12.3km. In the more congested areas, all of the differences in total vehicle kilometres and energy consumption became very marginal when the effects on the whole network were considered because of the increased emissions arising from congestion associated with a central location.

2.4.17 Only the model which was available for the less congested area considered has a public transport sub-model. In this case, the total time and money costs of users of car travel are very much lower than those of public transport users. Those with a car available tend to use it, regardless of their trip destination. However, the simulation for the other area does produce a much higher proportion of short trips in the central location option, implying greater potential scope for transfer to non-motorised modes such as walking and cycling.

2.4.18 Actual data for one of the case study areas on mode of arrival at "fringe-of-centre" and out-of-town retail warehouses indicate that, although the proportion of car-borne shoppers for all centres is high, the proportion of non-car borne shoppers is highest at the "fringe-of-centre" stores. Similarly, many of the recently developed out-of-town centres, such as Merry Hill in the Black Country, and the Meadow Hall Centre in Sheffield, are clearly designed to maximise accessibility by car.[64] This is reflected in their low number of public transport trips compared with traditional centres. The observed car dependency of new peripheral facilities no doubt largely reflects the fact that non-motorised modes are less likely to be a feasible means of travel to such outlets. This is a factor which conventional transport models cannot properly allow for. There is also the difficulty of serving a diffused pattern of trips by public transport to a single outlet, however large.

2.4.19 The simulations did, however, indicate that in some cases the locations on orbital routes involved higher average speeds. When account is taken of the greater accessibility of such locations to populations beyond the modelled urban areas, it is clear that they may well be preferred as locations by operators, even before considerations such as the availability of large sites and land costs are brought into the equation.

Public Services

2.4.20 A transport model-based simulation was carried out to compare the scenario of a single, large (400 bed) hospital in a central location with four smaller (100 bed) hospitals located to serve local centres of population. The district hospital option performs better in terms of distance travelled and fuel consumption. However, the differences are less than 1% and in practice it is considered that the outcome would be heavily dependent on the extent to which the district hospitals develop patterns of specialisation to serve the wider urban area, rather than simply providing general services to their local populations.

2.4.21 To explore these issues further, and to give explicit consideration to the potential role of public transport, a desk exercise was carried out for the West Midlands County comparing the options of a single central hospital in central Birmingham, a single non-central facility based on a peripheral site, and a network of district hospitals. Modal split assumptions were based on the feasibility of use of public transport from different areas and data from the NTS on the relationship between distance travelled and probability of use of different modes. The exercise suggests the district provision option would involve only 53% of the total travel associated with the single, central option and 49% of the car travel. A single non-central facility performs worse on both criteria. Again, the superiority of the district provision pattern would be undermined to the extent that specialisation and/or choice between district facilities develop.

Neighbourhood Structure

2.4.22 As part of the neighbourhood case studies work a postal survey was conducted to identify the particular characteristics of neighbourhood centres which contribute to their vitality and use by local residents. To keep the work manageable and to achieve good response rates the surveys primarily focused on retailing facilities. But many of the conclusions have a significantly wider application. The significance of neighbourhood issues is highlighted by the responses: an average of 96% of residents use their local centre at least weekly and 44% use them daily. The key points to arise and the associated conclusions, which are broadly in accordance with prior expectations, are summarised below:

- **The importance of different factors in determining usage of local centres:** Convenience and the range of facilities offered emerge as the dominant factors determining usage of local centres. Public transport links, the availability of parking and opportunities to make multi-purpose trips emerge as less important, but still significant, factors. The most utilised local facilities are food shops, followed by newsagents/stationers, with financial services/ post office and medical services also emerging as of some importance. People who visit local centres do so much more frequently than they use non-local centres. The latter assume much more importance in relation to durables shopping. Differences in the size and attraction of centres, to the extent that they help to determine the frequency and nature of trip patterns observed, also influence the mode of travel;

- **Distance and frequency of use:** As noted above, a clear relationship emerges between distance from a centre and the frequency of its use, with average distances to centres used on a daily basis being much shorter than those to centres used less frequently. Relative distance to the local and competing non-local centres is also important;

- **Mode of travel and journey distance:** Across the sample as a whole, some 43% of trips to local centres are made by car, 41% by bus and only 14% on foot or by bicycle. However, there are some clear relationships between distance and probability of use of different modes. In particular, walking is largely confined to trips of less than 1km, with motorised modes dominating longer trips. Thus, taken as a whole, the analysis shows that walking, at 53% for journeys to local and non-local centres, is the dominant mode for trips up to 1.6 kms, followed by car at 29%. For trips between 1.6 and 5 kms in length, the car becomes marginally the dominant mode (44%), followed by bus (43%) and walking (12%). The relationship between distance and mode of travel is shown in Table 11; and

- **Factors affecting choice of mode:** As noted in Section 2.2, socio-economic factors, in as far as they relate to levels of car ownership, can be a significant influence on modal choice. Population density also emerges as an important influence on travel behaviour at the neighbourhood level. This is reflected in the comparison of different neighbourhoods within each of the individual urban case study areas, where car usage is lower in the more dense neighbourhoods, even where levels of car ownership and occupational structures are broadly comparable. However, when the eight neighbourhoods are considered as a group and other factors come into play, not surprisingly, the role of density becomes more blurred. Another important explanatory variable appears to be the drive-time catchment area. It is claimed by retail operators that their main turnover is generated from within a 20-minute catchment area.[65] Centres located on or near high-accessibility locations will, therefore, tend to attract a higher proportion of non-local trips which are more likely to be made by motorised forms of transport.

2.4.23 The wide variations in the frequency with which particular modes of travel are used further highlights the importance of the local factors discussed above. For example, for journeys to local centres between the neighbourhoods, car usage varies from 48% in Sutton Farm (Shrewsbury), and 45% in Vanburgh (Greenwich), to as little as 22% in St Pauls (Sandwell), and 24% in Lakedale (Greenwich). Usage of bus is negligible in the Shrewsbury and Greenwich neighbourhoods, but accounts for at least 33% of trips to local centres in all four Black Country neighbourhoods. Cycling is of minimal significance in all cases. The proportion of walk trips varies enormously from less than 10% in Charlemont (Sandwell) to more than 40% (Cherry Orchard, Shrewsbury; Lakedale, Greenwich).

Table 11: **Proportion of Total Trips by Mode and Distance Travelled to Local and Non-local Centres**

Distance Travelled (kms)	Proportion of Trips by Mode (%)					Total Trips	
	Car	Bus	Train	Walk	Cycle	no.	%
<1	11	4	-	63	19	385	22
1 - 1.6	16	12	-	20	27	275	16
1.6 - 5	38	42	-	15	27	574	33
5 - 8	27	35	32	1	27	408	23
8 - 16	6	6	62	1	-	86	5
16+	2	1	6	-	-	16	1
Total	**100**	**100**	**100**	**100**	**100**		**100**
Total Trips no.	661	591	19	447	26	1,744[1]	-
Total Trips %	38	34	1	26	1	-	100

Source: *Neighbourhood Travel Surveys, 1992*
Notes: (1) This total includes information on more than one response per questionnaire.

2.4.24 Surprisingly, distance does not appear to be a major factor explaining these differences. It is difficult to discern clear influences on modal choice at the local level due to the number and variety of factors involved and the inter-relationships which exist between them.

2.4.25 Car usage is clearly related to car ownership. However, this relationship is complicated by the deterrent effects of congestion, particularly in London. Thus, although car ownership is much higher in Lakedale (Greenwich) than St Pauls (Sandwell), usage is broadly comparable. The low level of bus usage and correspondingly high proportion of walk trips in Shrewsbury and Greenwich may well reflect the attractive opportunities for walking in the former and, again, the deterrent effects of congestion on all forms of motorised travel in the latter. The Black Country districts fall somewhere in between these two extremes with lower densities and less congestion than Greenwich - which would tend to encourage greater use of motorised forms of transport - but more extensive public transport services -and possibly less attractive opportunities for walking - than Shrewsbury. The Black Country sample also contained a relatively high proportion of retired persons who benefit from concessionary bus fares.

2.4.26 These results illustrate the importance of design and local environmental characteristics. Further evidence on the potential for public transport provision and design to influence travel behaviour can be drawn from the experience of the new towns.

- **Runcorn** - New towns have not in general placed a strong emphasis on public transport provision. However, Runcorn was specifically designed to encourage public transport usage. A study of the Runcorn Busway by TRRL in 1976 indicated that a modal split of 50:50 between bus and car for journeys to work within the town was being achieved.[66] However, this was not due to car owners being attracted to the Busway as was hoped, but due to the lack of choice for many people who did not have a car available (50% of households). No recent data is available to confirm subsequent trends, although the indications are that the share of public transport has fallen but remains relatively high. Interestingly, it is understood that the developer for the latest major phase of expansion did not wish to incorporate an extension of the busway into the scheme.

- **International Comparisons** - recent work contrasts patterns of travel demand in Milton Keynes and Almere in the Netherlands.[67] Whilst Milton Keynes was designed around a 'grid' of dual-carriageway roads with the dispersal of traffic generating land uses, Almere, as well as being built to a higher density, incorporates segregated busways, cycleways and walkways with fairly extensive traffic calming measures. Comparisons of travel patterns in the two towns reveal:

  — 69% of all recorded trips in Milton Keynes were made by car; the figure for Almere was 43%;
  — bus trips were identical at 6% each;
  — the level of walk trips were 17% for Milton Keynes and 21% for Almere; and
  — over a quarter of all trips in Almere were made by cycle compared with just 6.2% in Milton Keynes.

Because of differences in national culture and uncertainties about how far differences in socio-economic characteristics may be involved, such comparisons should be treated with caution. However, they do indicate the potential role of land-use patterns in influencing or at least accommodating differences in travel behaviour.

2.4.27 The neighbourhood survey and other studies of pedestrian behaviour indicate that the environmental factors of most concern to pedestrians are the danger posed by traffic, followed by the level of emissions and noise pollution. Pedestrian priority and related traffic management and calming measures can help improve safety and, hence, encourage walking.[68] A number of towns have developed segregated pedestrian routes. Experience in Cumbernauld and Stevenage shows that such networks can help reduce accident rates.[69] The evidence supports the view that the various measures for pedestrian safety are more effective when implemented as part of a comprehensive plan rather than as isolated measures.[70]

2.4.28 Other studies have also argued that the combination of cycle routes with measures - such as traffic calming - that improve safety and security for cyclists can help shift motorised trips to cycle, particularly if action is focused upon flat and relatively dense towns and cities where the potential for cycling is greatest.[71]

Regional Structure

Level of Urbanisation

2.4.29 The evidence on the roles of density and population size reviewed above highlights the general point that, other things being equal, the concentration of a region's population in relatively dense, reasonably large urban areas is likely to be the most efficient outcome in terms of transport emissions. Indeed, as indicated in Section 2.2 above, the effects of density and urbanisation are statistically indistinguishable at the regional level.

Self-Containment

2.4.30 Travel generally is likely to be minimised to the extent that urban areas are able to achieve a high degree of self-containment. The presumption is that this will be promoted by each urban area having a reasonable balance of population and employment, as well as a wide range of facilities. In fact, the attempts statistically to relate travel demand in the urban case study areas to measures of self-containment and/or commuting flows proved unsuccessful.

2.4.31 It is also reasonable to assume that urban areas are more likely to achieve a high level of self-containment the greater their physical separation. This is supported by studies of the new towns. After achieving a high initial level of self-containment, peaking in the mid 1960s, new towns - particularly in the South East - appear to have become significantly less self-contained in recent years. New towns with reasonable access to major cities have increasingly become a source of medium to long distance commuting.[72] This reflects both the growth in commuting to London over the 1980s, which was associated with the growth in highly-paid service employment opportunities, and the widening of areas of housing and job search in areas of Southern England more generally. However, as settlements become more distant from London, or more remote generally, the level of self-containment tends to become higher. The implications are that free-standing towns of a reasonable size - sufficient to support a large number of employment opportunities, a range of social facilities and a good public transport system - are likely to be relatively self-contained and, therefore, energy-efficient forms of development.

Urban Containment

2.4.32 Particular issues arise in relation to the effect on the dispersion of population and travel demand of policies that contain the outward spread of the major urban areas. This issue is particularly pertinent in the South East Region where constraints on housing development near London were associated, particularly in the mid 1980s, with an outward shift in population, apparently driven by a combination of the pattern of housing opportunities, house-price differentials and relatively low real travel costs to London from the Outer South East and surrounding counties. It would be wrong to see this as simply a matter of Central London commuters moving further out, although this was a factor. Much of the movement and the associated growth in travel involved shorter-distance radial movement by those working in Outer London and the Inner South East, or resulted from migrants from other regions moving to take up jobs in the South East.[73]

2.4.33 Evidence to support the view that development constraints in the Inner South East contributed to wider travel growth in the South East is available from a range of sources.

- The observed rapid growth in the ring of counties surrounding the Inner South East in recent years. Population growth has been particularly rapid in Buckinghamshire, Cambridgeshire, and Northamptonshire. The evidence is that a significant proportion of new housing in counties in the South East is purchased by inmigrants from London and adjoining counties.[74] There is also an observed growth in longer-distance commuting to London;[75] and

- The gradient of house-price differentials shows a pattern of decline with increased distance and reduced accessibility to the Inner South East. Other work has indicated that the observed pattern of house-price differentials is broadly consistent with what would be expected based on the capitalised value of differences in generalised travel costs to London.[76]

Effects of the Green Belt and Urban Containment

2.4.34 To explore these issues further in isolation from the complex, and specific issues in the South East, it is useful to compare travel-to-work patterns for Coventry - one of the urban case study areas, which has an approved Green Belt varying from 4 to 10km wide - with two broadly comparable cities - Hull and Leicester - which do not have Green Belts (although the surrounding areas of both cities are subject to countryside policies that also constrain growth). Table 12 summarises the key characteristics of each city and Table 13 shows the distribution of journey-to-work trips by distance band for the three cities.

2.4.35 Average distances travelled to workplaces were highest in Coventry (7.1km), followed by Leicester (7.0km) and Hull (6.6km), despite the fact that Coventry is the smallest urban area and has the highest density. More significantly, the low proportion of the city's journey-to-work trips in the 5-9 km band, combined with the high proportion in the 10-19km band, is clearly consistent with the hypothesis that one of the effects of peripheral development constraints is to displace development to more distant locations and to increase travel demand.

Summary

2.4.36 The centralisation of employment and other trip-attracting activities has the effect of increasing the use of public transport for work and non-work trips. At least part of this effect represents the transfer of trips which, under other land-use patterns, would be undertaken by car. Centralisation may well, however, add to journey lengths, at least in relation to travel to work.

2.4.37 Whilst polycentric urban structures create

49

Table 12 **Key Characteristics of Selected Urban Areas**

City	Population (000s)	Radial Extent (kms)	Density (pph)	SEG Manual	Group Non-Manual	No car %
Leicester	369	7	25.7	52.2	42.6	35.1
Coventry	309	6	27.3	52.4	43.0	35.3
Hull	330	8	26.5	52.8	43.7	44.7

Source: Census of Population, 1981.

Table 13 **Travel-To-Work Distances for Selected Urban Areas**

	Less than 5 km	5-9 km	10-19 km	More than 20km
Leicester	60.0	25.7	8.9	5.5
Hull	57.9	29.7	8.4	4.0
Coventry	59.9	23.3	11.7	5.2

Source: Census of Population, 1981.

the potential for more travel efficient urban forms, there is no real evidence that this potential is likely to be realised in current circumstances. Evidence from the study simulations, however, does suggest that concentrating development in existing centres, rather than creating new ones, is likely to be more efficient from an emissions perspective (2.4.5 to 2.4.13).

2.4.38 The study simulations and also evidence from other studies suggests that intermixing residential and employment uses within a particular urban zone makes a negligible difference to distance travelled or modal choice. Intermixing is unlikely to have a short-term impact on reducing emissions from transport (2.4.14-2.4.15).

2.4.39 Considerations in the case studies of the travel demand implications of locating major retail developments indicated that central locations were associated with shorter trips and overall reductions in travel demand. However, the differences when compared with non-central locations were not large and the results were sensitive to local road network conditions (2.4.16-2.4.19).

2.4.40 At the neighbourhood level the survey results indicate that easy access to a neighbourhood centre, with a good range of facilities, can reduce travel to major centres. Distance is a key factor determining whether people walk or use motorised transport. Whilst walking is the predominant method of travel for very short trips, few trips in excess of 3 km are made on foot. Design which creates an attractive, safe environment for walking and cycling can also encourage use of non-motorised forms of travel (2.4.22-2.4.28).

2.4.41 At the regional level the degree of urbanisation is a major determinant of travel. A balance of population, employment and other activities is judged likely to help promote self-containment, although no definitive evidence is available (2.4.29). Self-containment will also be promoted if urban centres are sufficiently distant to discourage routine day-to-day travel between them (2.4.30-2.4.31). Evidence indicates that urban containment policies have led to some dispersal of population and increased journey-to-work lengths for certain groups, probably adding to total travel to some degree (2.4.32-2.4.35).

2.5 Transport Infrastructure and Development Pressures

Introduction

2.5.1 The impact of transport infrastructure on development pressures is not well understood, not least because very few systematic, longitudinal, ex-post assessments have been undertaken of major projects in the UK. The notable, published exception in the UK is the Tyne and Wear Metro, but the depressed local property market in the area of assessment and the specific nature of the project makes it difficult to draw general lessons.[77] A wider range of evidence is available from continental Europe and the United States, but its transferability to the UK context is open to debate.

2.5.2 It is difficult in any assessment to separate out those changes which would have occurred anyway from those which were specifically caused by a change in transport facilities. It is apparent too, in many cases, that the observed results of new transport infrastructure in development terms are to some extent a consequence of planning policy responses by local authorities. For example, in areas where development interest is limited, public authorities are often anxious to capitalise on the opportunity to offer high-quality, well-accessed sites. Where, as is often the case, there are few large, high-quality sites in the area, it then becomes very difficult to distinguish the effects of the provision of good large greenfield sites from the changes in patterns of accessibility associated with the new infrastructure. Conversely, in other instances - such as areas around the M25 - there is often a strong policy resistance to large-scale development in the vicinity of the infrastructure and the only evidence to assess its potential development effects is indirect - for example, retail rentals, house-price data for the limited amount of existing property nearby and the number and type of planning applications.

2.5.3 The evidence produced and assembled in the course of the study on local and strategic rail improvements, urban and interurban road links, and orbital roads and bypasses is reviewed in turn below.

Rail Improvements

2.5.4 There is evidence that firms are becoming more interested in the potential of rail for longer-distance freight movements. However, the major development effects of rail schemes in the UK have arisen from their impact on housing markets in areas which offer potential commuting opportunities to major urban centres, particularly London.

2.5.5 Previous approaches to estimating the significance of such effects have focused on the impacts of service improvements in increasing local house prices in commuting areas. Policy permitting, price increases would be expected to be followed in later years by increased rates of housing development. The methodology has involved direct comparisons of price movements within areas affected by improvements with price movements in control areas and regional average increases. Additionally, use has been made of simple statistical modelling techniques.[78]

2.5.6 The evidence indicates that rail improvements have some effect on boosting house prices, particularly in potential commuter areas in the South East and West Midlands. For a number of the areas and improvements considered there is evidence of substantial, above-average increases in house prices in the years when major improvements in services were introduced. The areas include: St Albans, Luton and Bedford (1978), Ipswich (1987) and Worcester (both in 1983 and 1987, when services to Birmingham were improved). In a number of statistical models the scale of the impact is such that standard statistical tests of significance are met.[79]

2.5.7 People generally trade travel costs and house prices in their choice of where to live and work. Rail improvements will tend to reduce the costs, increase travel distance associated with commuting and increase housing demand in the areas of impact. Since the change in the supply of new housing in response to price changes will be low in the short run, the process of inmigrant commuters bidding for the available supply of housing will tend to increase prices. This "capitalises" the benefits of improved accessibility in local house prices. The extent of this effect, and how far it persists over the long term, is likely to depend on two factors:

- how far the planning system and other factors permit the supply of housing in the area of impact to grow over the longer term to meet the increased demand; and

- the size of the potential inmigrant commuter market relative to the potential local housing supply.

The problem for many planning authorities over the 1980s, when commuting to Central London grew rapidly, was that the scale of the potential inmigrant commuter market was so large that the capacity, in any one area, to dampen house-price increases by permitting higher levels of development, became very limited.

2.5.8 Studies of rail schemes elsewhere in Europe and in North America has also indicated that they may have significant effects in facilitating the dispersal of population within wider city regions.[80] Studies have also suggested the following:

- Major rapid transport improvements have been important inducements to intensified developments near stations both in Central Business Districts and in outlying districts, although only when supported by other economically-favourable forces. Some recent major commuter rail improvements have been found to have led to significant land-use intensification, but evidence on light rail has been less conclusive;[81]

- There is little evidence that rapid transit improvements have led to any extra overall growth in the urban economy or in the population of cities as a whole - although these issues are inherently difficult to assess. The impacts may have been merely shifts within city regions rather than net increases in land values or economic activity. The study into the longer-term effects of the Tyne and Wear Metro concluded that *"land use and property markets have been little affected and that Metro had little*

or no effect on the pattern of housing development".[82] However, as noted above, the depressed market context limits the wider significance of this conclusion;

- The timing of land-use impacts seems heavily dependent on general economic conditions and is, therefore, difficult to isolate from wider patterns of change. A detailed study was carried out into planning permissions for office development in the catchment area of the Victoria Line which added 11 km of new underground railway in London in 1969. Using a different underground line as a control, it was found to be almost impossible to separate out the stimulus effect of office development given by the opening of the new line from those office developments which would have taken place anyway due to other market forces;[83] and

- Previous research has also identified that the level of impact of rail schemes is influenced by a range of factors, including: local planning authority policies; development trends and forces; land availability; and, the social and physical characteristics of the area.[84]

2.5.9 The general evidence is consistent with the view that transit schemes can have a significant influence on localised economic development in urban areas, where they are supported by positive development incentives, co-ordinated land-use and transport planning measures and a market context that is reasonably favourable. Thus, opportunities exist to utilise these influences for the purpose of reducing overall transport emissions.

Urban and Inter-Urban Road Schemes

2.5.10 Public authorities within the UK have typically given high priority to road schemes in the development of major urban regeneration initiatives. Many of the Urban Development Corporations (UDCs), for example, have given proposals for new urban spine roads a central place in their area strategies. The basis for this is the belief that improved access, in combination with site assembly and reclamation, can provide development opportunities competitive with those offered by peripheral locations. Consultations with the development industry and local authorities indicate that this view of the importance of such schemes is widely shared. However, none of these major schemes has reached the point where ex-post analysis can be undertaken. When evaluations are made, there will clearly be difficulty in disentangling the effects of improved road accessibility from the associated initiatives by the UDCs.

2.5.11 Evidence reviewed during the course of the study indicates that the nature of the development impacts resulting from major highway developments again depends, to a large extent, upon the interaction of three factors: [85]

- **Market Context** - the extent and pattern of existing development pressures and the degree to which the locations of development have previously been constrained by problems of accessibility;

- **Local Context** - consequent changes are influenced by the physical location and the prevailing socio-economic characteristics of an area which determine its suitability in market terms for different types of development; and

- **Policy Context** - the extent of any designated areas and protected landscapes and the attitude of the local planning authorities toward new development.

2.5.12 Thus, as noted by the Leitch Committee, accessibility is a necessary but not a sufficient condition for development interest.[86] This view is confirmed in a number of reviews of the empirical literature which have subsequently been undertaken, including one on the impact of transport projects on inner cities.[87]

2.5.13 The potential influence of new inter-urban routes can be illustrated by the case of the recently completed M40. In the period leading up to the opening of the motorway extension a considerable amount of speculative development took place. Surveys indicate a substantial rise in relative land values during the 1980s. Between 1987 and 1989, land prices on the motorway fringe around Banbury increased tenfold to nearly £2 million per hectare.[88] This activity anticipated future demand associated with improved accessibility. In general, the emphasis has been on offices and business uses, with little new industrial space. There have also been proposals for new settlements, such as Stone Bassett in Oxfordshire.

2.5.14 More recently, land values have declined and many of the schemes which have gone ahead are finding difficulties attracting occupiers. The availability of substantial levels of office floorspace during and since the late 1980s in the South East may continue to depress rental growth for some time to come. However, although development in the area has slowed, the pipeline contains a large number of schemes awaiting an economic upturn.

2.5.15 The evidence from major development corridors, such as the M4, is that development interest often spreads out from major centres, particularly London, along major radial routes as both firms and people move outwards in response to cost pressures and/or constraints on their operation or expansion in their original, and often preferred, location. Thus, for example, many of the firms in towns such as Basingstoke and Reading originated in West London. Levels of development interest in areas such as Newbury are also closely related to the extent of the development and labour market constraints applying in towns closer to London.[89]

2.5.16 Analyses of major highway schemes comparable to that of the work on rail improvements have not been undertaken. However, the indications are that, in combination with restrictive planning policies in counties around London, the development of the motorway system has provided a powerful stimulus to the observed decentralisation of population to counties outside the Inner South East. This poses challenges to the planning system in so far as the process of decentralisation is linked to increases in travel demand. Improvements to the road network (particularly through new road building) pose similar challenges in so far as they considerably extend the potential availability of sites with good road access.

Orbital Routes and Bypasses

2.5.17 Orbital routes, which are a comparatively recent phenomenon, have now been built or are planned for several major UK cities. Their primary transport rationale is to accommodate strategic traffic movements and hence free capacity on intra-urban routes, thus also securing important local environmental improvements. In practice they also radically alter the relative accessibility of a wide range of locations and appear to influence the pattern of demand for development significantly. They increase the attractiveness and accessibility of housing with reasonable access and extend the effective travel to work, and areas of job search, for households in their vicinity. As far as economic activities are concerned, orbital routes are particularly beneficial to industrial and distribution activities, they can accommodate 'just-in-time' deliveries and enable access to wide labour markets.

2.5.18 In the West Midlands, for example, proposals for a Northern and Western Relief Road will provide an orbital route of full motorway standards around the conurbation. The following broad impacts are evident:

- **Accessibility** - the completion of the proposed motorway box, together with the M40, will adjust further the balance of advantage in accessibility in favour of peripheral areas and free-standing towns beyond the metropolitan area;

- **Development Pressures** - a number of related proposals for business parks have been received for land in the vicinity of major junctions, including those located in designated Green Belt areas;

- **Rental Levels** - the anticipated changes in accessibility, coupled with prevailing planning constraints, mean that office rentals on premises in locations, such as around the existing M42, are comparable to those in Birmingham and Solihull centres and are well above those in other parts of the conurbation; and

- **Policy Responses** - it is clear that a number of local authorities see the new parts of the motorway box as an important economic development opportunity. Interestingly, too, the Secretary of State's Planning Guidance accepts the provision off up to 300 hectares of land for industrial development on the periphery of the conurbation. Site selection will be related to decisions on the Northern Relief Road and the Western Orbital Route.[90]

2.5.19 The precise impacts associated with the construction of orbital routes clearly vary according to the particular context in question and the influence of other factors, including the market context, planning policies and the quality of related transport infrastructure. Nevertheless, orbital routes are not in themselves a mechanism which can entirely explain the pressures for decentralisation. However, once built - usually in response to the problem of congestion - they can be a powerful influence contributing to the dispersal of economic activities, particularly in areas where economic development is a priority objective. Furthermore, they lead to travel patterns that cannot easily be replicated by public transport.

2.5.20 In many areas where pressures for decentralisation are strong, it is difficult for certain activities which would most benefit from such locations - particularly distribution activities - to compete with developments such as business parks. This is particularly so because the motivations for occupiers to move to business parks include factors such as corporate prestige as well as accessibility.

2.5.21 At more local levels research has examined how the construction of by-passes affected land-use and development patterns in 32 towns.[91] This work concluded that the effects of by-pass construction on land use and development were negligible relative to other factors - including market context, planning policies, land ownership and site characteristics. This difference in experience compared with orbital routes

around major urban areas is interesting. It probably reflects the easier opportunities for, and reduced interest in, substantial office development in most smaller towns, and the reduced significance of congestion-related costs in relation to central locations in smaller urban areas.

2.5.22 The main impacts identified concerned the location of warehousing, which tended to locate near by-pass access points, particularly if this was part of a national through route. Peripheral sites near by-pass interchanges were also attractive to superstores, although the pressures for their development had, for the most part, been successfully resisted by local planning authorities. Considerable development pressures were created in some cases where by-pass routes are close to the periphery of the urban area. However, a route which passes close to an urban area can also be used to restrict further development, as authorities are usually reluctant to breach the strongly physical barrier of a by-pass.

Summary

2.5.23 The major development effects of rail schemes in the UK have arisen from their impact on housing markets in areas which offer potential commuting opportunities to major urban centres (2.5.4). There is also evidence that transit schemes can have a significant influence on localised economic development in urban areas (2.5.9).

2.5.24 The development impacts resulting from major highway developments depend upon the interaction of property market and socio-economic factors and the policy context. The development of the motorway system has stimulated decentralisation and considerably extended the potential availability of sites with good road access (2.5.16). Orbital routes around major urban centres can also contribute to the dispersal of economic activities and lead to travel patterns that cannot easily be replicated by public transport (2.5.19). In contrast the construction of by-passes has had relatively minor impacts on development trends (2.5.21-2.5.22). However, new access roads for particular sites can have important localised impacts on development.

2.5.25 Overall the limited number of studies of the impact of transport infrastructure projects on development in the UK, and the evidence that the nature of the impacts depends on a series of contextual factors, warns against simple or general conclusions. In practice, responses by planning authorities to new infrastructure are an important factor in the observed association between infrastructure projects and development. Leaving this issue aside, road - and in some case commuter rail - schemes can significantly affect development pressures in one of two circumstances:

- firstly, and most importantly, where they remove barriers for movement between an area where land prices are relatively high and the market is buoyant, but development is constrained, and another where land prices are lower and more development opportunities are available; and

- secondly, where they significantly change the relative accessibility of different parts of an urban area (2.5.18).

The resultant development in both cases is likely to represent a mix of pure displacement of activity from one area to another and net additional activity, with the precise mix depending on the extent to which accessibility and other constraints represent a barrier to development in the total area under consideration.

E

Part III The Implications for Policy

3.1 Introduction

3.1.1 The purpose of this part of the report is to draw out the main implications of the study findings for planning policies in the UK.

3.1.2 Section 3.2 considers the implications relevant to those land-use factors which can potentially influence travel behaviour, including: density; settlement population size; regional structure; urban structure; and neighbourhood structure. Responses to the development pressures caused by transport infrastructure are also reviewed.

3.1.3 Section 3.3 considers the potential role of policies complementary to planning: parking controls; park-and-ride schemes; pedestrian priority and traffic calming measures; cycle priority measures; and public transport priority measures, drawing on the study evidence.

3.1.4 Finally, Section 3.4 puts forward a number of 'tools' that could help the planning process achieve the objective of reducing transport emissions. These are particularly relevant given that the study findings strongly indicate that the planning policies required to reduce travel demand will vary from locality to locality.

3.1.5 The main planning policies that emerge as likely to contribute to reductions in transport emissions have each been assessed against a number of criteria to identify, in particular, the extent to which they are likely to complement or conflict with other planning (and other public policy) objectives and the major risks and uncertainties in the light of market trends and other evidence. The detailed findings of this assessment are given in Appendix 2.

3.2 Planning Policy Options

Introduction

3.2.1 This section of the report considers the implication for planning policies of the study findings concerning: density, settlement size, regional structure, urban structure (and centralisation) and neighbourhood structure. It also assesses the planning responses required to the development of transport infrastructure that will help reduce overall transport emissions. A more detailed assessment of the planning policies put forward is given in Appendix 2.

Density

3.2.2 Section 2.2 concluded that higher residential densities within settlements are likely to be associated with reductions in travel demand and the encouragement of shifts towards emissions-efficient modes. However, the extent of any reduction and modal shift was complicated by factors such as location and income and possible adaptive responses. Certainly, simple comparisons between the transport energy efficiency of settlements of different densities are likely to be a poor guide to the actual level of transport emission reductions which is possible.

3.2.3 Planning policies can encourage higher densities through:

- imposing minimum density standards on new development;

- encouraging development within existing urban boundaries (on vacant, derelict or underused land for example); and

- encouraging higher density development, or redevelopment, at or near to public transport nodes or within corridors well-served by public transport.

3.2.4 Such policies are broadly consistent with existing planning policies and their implementation would be unlikely to induce major conflicts with other current planning objectives. Amongst the groups most likely to benefit from such policies are those living in urban areas without access to a private car figure prominently. The implementation of such policies will depend critically on effective co-ordination of planning and public transport measures.

Settlement size

3.2.5 Section 2.3 concludes that, in most cases, the dispersal of population from major centres has been associated with increases in travel demand and a modal shift away from public transport. It is also evident that smaller settlements (those with populations of less than 50,000 and particularly very small settlements) are characteristically less transport emissions-efficient than larger settlements. However, the relationships between settlement size and transport emissions are complicated by differences in levels of car ownerships and particular settlement patterns.

3.2.6 Planning policies can have an influence on settlement size, but this influence is limited, in the UK context, by the low level of overall population growth. The main relevant planning policies include:

- the location of the bulk of new housing land in existing larger settlements;

- constraints over the incremental expansion of small settlements, particularly those likely to accommodate relatively long-distance commuters and not benefiting from good public transport access; and

- where new settlements are to be developed, locating them away from larger settlements.

3.2.7 These planning policies are broadly consistent with existing policies. The proposed policies are unlikely to result in marked impacts on different groups, although policies of constraint in 'popular' settlements will tend to advantage those already owning property in these areas to the detriment of first-time buyers.

Regional structure

3.2.8 Section 2.4 stressed that the extent of urbanisation within regions was a major determinant of travel demand. It also pointed out that travel demand is likely to be lower where there is a balance of employment and other activities within individual urban areas and reasonable geographic separation between centres. Both of these factors encourage self containment and hence can reduce transport emissions.

3.2.9 As with the planning policies concerned with settlement size, in the context of low levels of population growth, the short-term impact of planning policies on regional structure is limited. However, the following policies are relevant:

- urban regeneration that encourages improvements in the balance of employment, other economic activities and residential development at the urban level; and

- the expansion of urban areas in ways that take advantage of existing public transport infrastructure and create the potential to support new services. (The policies in 3.2.6 are also relevant in this context.)

3.2.10 The extent to which such policies are likely to be in conflict within other planning objectives will vary between areas. For example, in some circumstances, the most appropriate form of expansion for a particular locality in terms of transport emissions-efficiency could be a linear expansion, along the line of a public transport corridor, but intruding into a designated green belt. Nevertheless, in broad terms, such planning measures are consistent with the planning objectives evident in recent years.

3.2.11 As with some of the other planning measures put forward in this section, there are potential detrimental impacts on traffic congestion. However, as discussed below, to the extent that the planning measures enable travel to be accommodated by public transport or other emissions-efficient modes, then the effects of road congestion, particularly in urban areas, will at least be mitigated. No marked differential impacts upon different groups in the community are likely to result from these measures.

Urban structure and centralisation

3.2.12 Section 2.4 concludes that the centralisation of employment and other trip-generating activities (leisure, retail etc) has the effect of increasing the use of public transport (and hence reducing overall transport emissions) relative to less centralised structures. However, high levels of centralisation and the concentration of land uses are also associated with long-distance trips (and hence high overall travel). The evidence on the influence of polynuclear (multicentred) structures and the intermixing of land uses on transport emissions is less clear. Both create the potential for more transport energy-efficient urban structures, but this potential may not be realised in practice.

3.2.13 Planning policies can strongly influence the urban structure, centralisation and the intermixing of land uses, so as to create the potential to reduce emissions by, for example, encouraging the:

- focusing of trip-generating activities at high density in the central areas of towns and cities, which is particularly helpful if development is linked to public transport nodes, such as railway stations;

- "balancing" of growth of employment and population within settlements and the physical juxtaposition of employment and residential uses; and

- the retention and development of hierarchies of centres within urban areas, so as to enhance accessibility to local services.

3.2.14 Each of these planning policies is broadly consistent with existing planning objectives and practice. For example, in London strong emphasis has been given to the location of office developments close to the central railway stations. However, the extent to which planning authorities have been willing and able in practice to resist the pressures for decentralisation of office employment and activities, such as retailing, has clearly been variable. Such policies can help create the conditions within which transport demand can be met more readily by emissions-efficient modes.

Neighbourhood structure

3.2.15 It is worth stressing that a high proportion of all travel is essentially local and that a very high proportion of all trips are relatively short and on foot. As National Travel Survey data show, although walking accounts for a relatively small proportion of distance travelled, it accounts for over one-third of all passenger journeys. This illustrates the importance of walking in providing access to a variety of destinations. The review of evidence in Section 2.4 further indicates that proximity to local centres and design characteristics are important factors in encouraging their use, and again highlights the significance of walking and cycling for short journeys.

3.2.16 Planning policies can have a strong influence on neighbourhoods, particularly if they are linked with positive measures to influence investment in public facilities and amenities. The following planning policies would encourage the reduction of transport emissions:

- the encouragement of residential development in the vicinity of local centres;

- the location of public services in local centres to minimise overall associated travel;

- the provision of safe and convenient access for pedestrians and cyclists;

- the encouragement of investment in, and maintenance and improvement of, existing local centres;

- the encouragement of high design and local environmental standards; and

- the encouragement of the provision of local services in parallel with new residential development.

3.2.17 Each of these policy measures is consistent with existing planning objectives and is unlikely to induce impacts detrimental to other planning objectives. Implementation of the policy will clearly need to take account of the likely long-term viability of particular centres. Nevertheless, the measures have an important role to play in supporting and enhancing the high proportion of trips undertaken by non-car modes. The measures should complement urban regeneration initiatives by improving environmental quality and, hence, making urban areas more liveable and attractive.

Responding to the land-use pressures generated by new transport infrastructure

3.2.18 The analysis in Section 2.5 on the impact of transport infrastructure has two important implications for planning policies to reduce transport emissions:

- In circumstances where good quality transport links are available, policies of selective constraint on housing development are likely to lead to a separation between place of residence and the places at which economic activities are conducted, so increasing travel. This process appears to have been particularly evident in the South East where the combination of high London house prices and an extensive rail network has contributed to the phenomenon of long distance commuting; and

- In relation to issues of urban regeneration, and more generally, there are significant potential benefits to be secured from the co-ordination of land-use planning and major infrastructure provision.

3.2.19 Section 2.5 concluded that new transport infrastructure could, depending upon local planning policies:

- enable people to extend their housing location choice;

- improve the market prospects for development in particular locations; and

- profoundly influence, in the case of orbital road routes, the relative accessibility of peripheral as opposed to central locations.

3.2.20 These effects are potentially highly significant influences on transport emissions. If planning is to influence the overall level of emissions, these impacts need to be considered as part of the assessment of the transport infrastructure investment decision. Planning policies need to be developed that can respond to impacts, both detrimental and beneficial. Such policies include:

- measures to safeguard sites with high quality road access for land uses having an inherent 'economic need' for such sites (such as distribution and some forms of manufacturing); and

- measures to concentrate development in locations benefitting from improvements in public transport infrastructure and services.

3.2.21 The second of these measures is consistent with most existing planning policies. However, the importance ascribed by developers to public transport provision clearly depends on the ease of access by car to the area concerned and other aspects of the relative costs of using public and private transport. In the absence of price differentials favouring public transport, case study evidence suggests that the use of public transport can be encouraged by combining strict control over parking provision with a focus on development at sites located adjacent to key nodes on the public transport network.

3.2.22 There is greater scope for conflict in respect of the potential measures to safeguard - for goods transport-related activities - locations which benefit from the improvements in road access brought about by new road building, especially where these are located beyond the boundaries of existing urban areas. Two types of conflict are likely to arise. Firstly, such locations may be in green belt or otherwise subject to local environmental concerns. Secondly, the location may be subject to strong demand from relatively more employment-intensive business uses where a high proportion of employees would use the private car for journeys to work. In the latter case the significance attached to the achievement of local employment and economic objectives frequently appears to outweigh potential transport and environmental considerations.

Summary

Planning policies for reducing transport emissions

3.2.23 From the above discussion it is evident that the following planning policies individually, and more particularly in combination, are likely to contribute to reductions in transport emissions :

- The encouragement of high densities of development through minimum density standards and the focusing of development within existing urban boundaries;

- The concentration of development in settlements with the potential for self containment;

- The encouragement of balanced employment and residential development at the level of individual settlements and in localities within existing urban areas;

- The encouragement of development close to public transport nodes and in corridors well served by public transport;

- The centralisation of trip-attracting activities and the retention of hierarchies of centres that enable access to local services by walking and public transport;

- The enhancement of neighbourhood centres through design, maintenance and development control policies; and

- The safeguarding of sites benefitting from good road access for activities having an economic need for such locations.

3.2.24 **Settlement Pattern and Size.** The dispersal of population away from major centres and towards smaller settlements has been associated with increases in transport emissions. Planning policies can have a limited influence on settlement size and the reduction of emissions through:

- allocating the bulk of housing land within existing larger settlements;

- constraining development in small settlements; and

- where new settlements are to be developed, locating them away from major urban centres (3.2.5-3.2.7).

3.2.25 **Regional Structure.** The extent of urbanisation and the separation of urban areas within regions are major influences on travel demand. The planning policies that can influence these aspects of regional structure and hence transport emissions are:

- urban regeneration that encourages balanced growth of employment and residential development; and

- the expansion of urban areas in ways that improve the viability of public transport (3.2.9).

3.2.26 **Urban Structure.** The centralisation of employment and other trip-generating activities has the effect of increasing the use of public transport and reducing overall transport emissions relative to less centralised structures. Evidence on the intermixing of land uses is less clear. The planning policies which can influence urban structure, centralisation and the intermixing of land uses are:

- the focusing of activities at high density in the central areas of towns and cities;

- the balanced growth of employment and population; and

- the retention and development of hierarchies of centres within urban areas (3.2.11-3.2.14).

3.2.27 **Neighbourhood Structure.** The increased use of local facilities for shopping and services is likely to be associated with reductions in transport emissions as a high proportion of trips to local centres are short and undertaken on foot. Planning policies can influence the attractiveness, vitality and viability of local centres through, for example:

- encouraging nearby residential development;

- ensuring high design and local environmental standards; and

- influencing the location of public services to minimise overall associated travel (3.2.15-3.2.17).

3.2.28 **Transport infrastructure.** New transport infrastructure can, depending upon local planning policies, influence development trends. These trends can in turn influence the levels of transport emissions. The planning policies that can respond to these trends and reduce emissions include measures to:

- safeguard sites benefitting from high quality road access for land uses, such as distribution, which have an economic need for such sites; and

- measures to concentrate development in locations benefitting from improvements in public transport infrastructure and services (3.2.20).

3.2.29 Overall the analysis of evidence in Part II provides a basis for identifying a variety of planning policies that can contribute to reducing transport emissions. However, the applicability of the policies varies between areas and a combination or 'packages' of approaches will be required.

3.2.30 Since there is a strong measure of correspondence between the planning policies put forward and contemporary practice potential conflicts with other planning objectives are limited. Possible areas of tension identified include:

- the preservation of green belt and possible, selective urban expansion within transport corridors (3.2.10); and

- the safeguarding of well-accessed locations for uses 'needing' such locations and local economic or environmental considerations (3.2.19).

3.2.31 There are some significant conflicts between the planning policies put forward and current socio-economic trends. Policies to extend choice in the use of public services may also be at odds with measures to reduce overall travel demand. However, those without access to private cars are likely to be significant beneficiaries of the planning policies which seek to reduce transport emissions.

3.3 Planning and Complementary Measures

3.3.1 There are several measures closely related to planning which could help bring about reductions in transport emissions - especially through encouraging shifts to emissions-efficient modes. These include: parking controls; provision for park-and-ride facilities; pedestrian priority and other traffic-calming measures; cycle priority measures; and public transport priority measures.

Parking controls

3.3.2 Planning policies can influence parking provision in several ways, for example through:

- the application of **maximum** parking provision standards combined with parking restrictions on nearby streets in new non-residential developments;

- the application of **minimum** car parking standards in new residential development;

- the granting or refusal of planning permissions for public and private car parks, particularly in city and town centres; and

- the prevention or encouragement of the redevelopment of sites used for parking for alternative uses.

3.3.3 In concert with highway authorities, the planning process should be able to influence:

- pricing policies in publicly-owned car parks;
- the enforcement of parking restrictions; and
- overall levels of on and off-street parking provision.

3.3.4 However, as a planning measure, parking has limitations. For example, it is not possible to exert any precise control over overall supply; enforcement is difficult and expensive, and drivers' adaptive behaviour may include "searching" for spaces in non-restricted areas, adding to congestion and overall distance travelled. This latter effect was evident in one of the simulations. Parking controls are also ineffective in controlling - and in some circumstances may even encourage - through trips to uncontrolled destinations. Additionally, many drivers do not bear the direct costs of parking and the vast majority of car trips do not incur any parking charges. There is also a risk that parking availability may influence shoppers' choice between competing centres. Evidence also indicate that changes in parking charges may need to be very substantial in order to induce changes in travel behaviour.[92]

3.3.5 Nevertheless, there is evidence that parking controls can strongly influence travel behaviour,[93] for example:

- car parking policies can discourage car traffic from urban centres; and

- the availability of car parking influences modal choice.

The evidence from surveys of office developments in one of the case study London Boroughs identifies car-parking provision as a significant factor in the decision to use a car for the journey to work.[94]

3.3.6 In view of these conflicting considerations, parking policies need to be seen as a component within an overall policy package. Four measures seem most likely to be effective in reducing travel demand:

(i)   consistent limits agreed at a strategic level on overall car-parking provision in potentially competing town and suburban centres;

(ii)   pricing policies that inhibit travel by car for shopping and particularly commuting to town centres;

(iii)   specific limits in relation to developments in central areas served by public transport to restrict the provision of parking to the minimum necessary for operational purposes; and

(iv)   high standards of underground car parking in high-density residential development to provide maximum living space and to preserve road capacity and environmental quality.

Park-and-ride schemes

3.3.7   Planning can help enable the provision of park-and-ride schemes. In broad terms these can be divided into two types:

(i)   parking facilities provided at rail stations on radial routes serving major urban centres and patronised in large part by commuters; and

(ii)   parking provided on the fringes of urban areas or city centres and serviced by public transport to encourage transfers to bus or other modes as a town-centre traffic and environmental management measure.

3.3.8   Park-and-ride schemes have been assessed in terms of their use, the patronage they generate for public transport, the extent to which they enable higher-density development in town centres and their impact on congestion. A number of factors have influenced their success in relation to these criteria:

● location in relation to catchment area and main routes;

● overall distance from city centres; and

● design, publicity, security and the quality of public transport services. [95]

3.3.9   The impact on overall travel demand and hence transport emissions is not well documented, but is unlikely to be marked and may well vary according to local circumstances. There are three reasons for this. Firstly, park-and-ride facilities at main suburban rail routes may encourage the wider dispersal of commuters able to use those facilities for journey-to-work purposes. Secondly, overall journey length for short-distance trips to town centres may be increased through diversion to edge-of-town car parks. Thirdly, use may be confined to times of high demand.

3.3.10 Currently one of the most comprehensive schemes in operation is the park-and-ride scheme in Oxford. The service, as surveys in other towns also show, is highly popular with the public. On a typical weekday in 1990, about 3,000 cars entered the four car parks, rising to 4,000 on Saturdays. Since 1973, traffic flows into the city centre have remained broadly constant in contrast to national trends, although there has been an increase in traffic at the edge of the city. However, the park-and-ride system has enabled increasing numbers of people to get into the city centre without any substantial increase in flows on radial routes. This has also enabled valuable city centre land to be developed, as parking has been transferred from the centre to the edge of the city. [96]

3.3.11 Park-and-ride schemes, particularly those catering for town-centre shoppers and visitors, may have an important long-term role in reducing congestion and encouraging the use of emissions-efficient modes, not least through their role in enhancing environmental quality in and around urban centres.

Pedestrian priority and traffic calming measures

3.3.12 Planning can play a role in the identification and implementation of pedestrian priority and traffic calming measures. These include: pedestrian schemes for town centre and shopping areas; and limitations on road capacity and design features to reduce the speed of traffic in residential areas. Such measures have generated positive impacts in terms of:

● reducing pedestrian casualty rates; [97]

● increasing pedestrian and cycling activity;

● reducing traffic noise and traffic volumes in residential areas; and

● enhancing the turnover of shops which are afforded better environment and access through pedestrian schemes linked with good public transport provision; [98]

3.3.13 The neighbourhood case studies highlight the key importance of providing easily accessible facilities which do not entail time-consuming and tiring journeys, and which promote the potential for making multi-purpose trips. Safety is of particular concern to pedestrians and this issue can be addressed through a number of measures. Planning can play a role in the development of segregated pedestrian routes, particularly between residential areas and town centres. In some areas it may be possible to utilise existing linear space systems based on rivers, canals and disused railways. In new developments it is possible to incorporate specific design features to promote walking by reducing the amount of necessary road crossing, by for example, suitably planning the locations of homes in relation to activities and by routing traffic away from pedestrian areas.

3.3.14 Continental experience is also instructive in this respect. Measures used in German and Dutch cities aim to reduce vehicle speeds through a combination of physical measures - humps, tables, chicanes - and regulatory techniques to give priority to pedestrians at road intersections.[99]

3.3.15 In terms of the impact of pedestrian and traffic calming measures on overall travel demand and emissions there is no clear evidence and, in their own right, only modest impacts are likely. However, some shifts from car to walking and cycling could be anticipated for short trips and, coupled with an intensification of development and the provision of public transport, significant long-term benefits in this respect seem likely.

Cycle priority measures

3.3.16 Planning can play a significant role in the provision of cycleways and cycle priority measures through, for example, the safeguarding of existing routes and encouraging their provision in new developments. The proportion of travel by cycle has declined in Britain from 12% in 1952 to around 1%. However, the annual distance travelled has remained stable at around 5 billion km since 1968.[100] There exists the potential for more travel by cycle:

- three quarters of the population can cycle and 35% of households have at least one cycle;

- 75% of all journeys are less than 8km in length, but 61% of these trips are made by car;

- in many urban areas cycling can produce faster journey times than other modes, particularly buses;[101] and

- cycling is cheaper than any mode other than walking.

3.3.17 Against this, of course, are the problems of safety and security, terrain and weather. The impact on total transport emissions from increases in cycling in urban areas will be reduced because of the likelihood that many of the trips involved will be shifted from bus rather than car.[102] However, it has been estimated that if 20% of non-walk trips were carried out by cycle, a reduction of around 4 - 6% in transport-related CO_2 emissions could be achieved.[103] This is most likely to be achieved if:

- cycleway provision is combined with other measures that improve safety and security for cyclists, such as traffic calming;[104]

- action is focused on flat and relatively dense towns and cities, where the inherent potential for cycling is greatest;[105] and,

- cycle parking facilities are provided, particularly at educational institutions and public transport interchanges.

Public transport priority measures

3.3.18 Planning can make a contribution to public transport priorities through measures such as the reservation of road space for buses. The simulation undertaken for a free-standing city in the Midlands illustrated the effect of bus-priority measures on public transport usage. In this case, bus usage (in passenger kilometerage) was increased by 7% due to the reduction in bus journey times of about 25% induced by bus-priority measures. The impact of such measures is likely to be enhanced by traffic calming and park-and-ride facilities.

Summary

3.3.19 Complementary measures which could help bring about a reduction in transport emissions include: parking controls; provision of park-and-ride facilities; pedestrian priority and traffic calming measures; the provision of cycle priority measures; and public transport priority measures.

3.3.20 Four measures concerning parking are likely to be useful components of an overall policy package to reduce transport emissions:

- consistent limits agreed at a strategic level on overall car parking provision in potentially competing town and suburban centres;

- car parking pricing policies that inhibit travel by car for shopping and particularly commuting to town centres;

- specific limits on car parking in developments in central areas served by public transport; and

- high standards of underground parking in high-density residential developments (3.3.2-3.3.6).

3.3.21 Park-and-ride schemes have not been assessed in terms of their impact on overall transport emissions. However, they may have an important long-term role in reducing congestion and encouraging the use of emissions-efficient modes, not least through their role in enhancing environmental quality in and around urban centres (3.3.7-3.3.11).

3.3.22 There is no clear evidence that pedestrian and traffic calming measures will, by themselves, lead to reductions in transport emissions. However, they could contribute to shifts from car to walking and cycling for short trips and, coupled with the intensification of development and the provision of public transport significant long-term benefits in this respect seem likely (3.3.12-3.3.15).

3.3.23 The proportion of travel by cycle has declined in Britain although the annual distance travelled has remained stable. It has been estimated that if 20% of non walk trips were carried out by cycle a reduction of around 4-6% in transport emissions could be achieved. This could be encouraged by the provision of cycleways, cycle priority measures and cycle parking facilities (3.3.16 and 3.3.17).

3.3.24 Public transport priority measures can encourage shifts towards public transport and hence reductions in transport emissions. Planning can support these measures through, for example, reserving road space for buses (3.3.18).

3.3.25 Overall, planning is likely to have a greater impact on travel demand and the encouragement of emissions-efficient modes if it is coupled with other complementary measures. Planning can also contribute to the success of other measures. However, the assessment of other measures has tended to be in terms of patronage and modal choice rather than their impact on transport emissions.

3.4 Tools to Assist the Planning Process

3.4.1 It is evident from the discussion in Part II that there is a complex inter-play of factors which influence travel behaviour. The magnitude and, even in some cases, the direction of impact on travel demand of the planning measures put forward in this report will be dependent upon particular local circumstances. It will thus be necessary for local planning authorities to generate plans and decision-making criteria both consistent with the overall objective to reduce travel demand and closely tailored to local circumstances.

3.4.2 There are at least five types of tools that could assist in this process:

(i)   Strategic studies to assess the likely impacts on travel demand of different land-use allocations and transport investment at the regional and county levels;

(ii) Studies to provide a basis for land-use and other measures at the urban scale;

(iii) Assessments of travel impacts of individual new developments;

(iv) 'Demonstration' projects which, through careful monitoring, could provide wider lessons on measures to reduce travel demand; and

(v)   The definition of priority zones in the vicinity of new transport infrastructure.

Each tool is described briefly below.

Strategic studies at the regional and county levels

3.4.3 The purpose of these studies would be to explore the likely implications on overall travel demand of additional development taking place in alternative locations, with or without investments in transport infrastructure, and the management of competition between centres to attract the private motor car. The methodologies applied in the simulations used in this study provide a starting point. The studies would need to be informed by a clear hierarchy of aims, objectives and performance measures. Reduction in fuel consumption would represent the single most important evaluation criterion, but it could also be helpful to "cost" other impacts, such as infrastructure costs and congestion that could be affected by the alternative planning strategies. The output of such work commissioned by groupings of authorities, or by authorities individually, would help to inform the preparation of advice to the Secretary of State in regional or strategic planning guidance and the preparation of structure plans.

Studies at the urban or local level

3.4.4. Comparable long-term studies should be prepared at the urban or district level. These could be used to help set objectives and targets for reductions in travel demand for the urban area and could form an important component of the local plan preparation process. A key purpose would be to identify how, at the urban level, planning and other measures could help generate reductions in transport emissions. This would help make clear the long-term policy and infrastructure commitments necessary.

F

Assessment of the travel impacts of alternative locations for new development

3.4.5 Traffic impact assessments are important considerations in development control decisions. In the context of an objective to reduce transport emissions it is, however, more important that the impact of developments on overall travel is considered, rather than simply the effects on the transport network in the immediate vicinity of the development. Such tools would be most useful in circumstances where comparisons are being made between different locations for the same type of development. The simulations provide examples of how this can be done. More sophisticated approaches would involve greater consideration of where trips associated with particular new developments are likely to be drawn from in each case - perhaps using gravity model principles - and of the pattern of trips to the development which are likely to arise from outside the urban area. This work could provide valuable inputs into the preparatory stages of structure and local plans.

Demonstration projects

3.4.6 There are perhaps three types of demonstration projects that would, assuming they proved successful in practice, help encourage widespread implementation of planning approaches that would reduce transport emissions. They are:

(i) high-density development at transport nodes;

(ii) high-density, mixed-use developments within city and town centres well served by public transport and complemented by creative and intensive use of green space; and

(iii) concentration of employment uses at public transport interchanges.

3.4.7 Design competitions could be held, public private sectors partnerships formed to promote developments and schemes selected on the basis of likely reduction in overall transport emissions. Supportive initiatives could also be developed to help encourage other experiments in telematics, telephone shopping and deliveries of goods by emissions-efficient modes.

The definition of priority zones in the vicinity of new transport infrastructure

3.4.8 As discussed in Part II, the provision of transport infrastructure has important impacts on the accessibility of different locations and hence on the spatial pattern of land use demands. If planning authorities are to control the type and forms of development taking place in proximity to new or improved infrastructure, and if emphasis is to be placed on ensuring that land uses with strong need for freight goods access assume priority, then there would be merit in defining priority zones around new transport infrastructure - for example, near motorway intersections or near railway stations. These zones would assume particular priority within the planning process, with particular attention paid to the exclusion of activities which would derive benefits from such locations mainly through the accessibility they provide for car-borne employees.

Summary

3.4.9 There are five "tools" that would assist the land use planning process to generate strategies, plans, policies and proposals, which will reduce/minimise the need to travel. They are:

- strategic studies to assess the impacts and costs and benefits of alternative land use and transport strategies at the regional and county levels (3.4.3);

- studies to provide a basis for the co-ordination of land use and other measures at the urban scale (3.4.4);

- techniques to assess the transport as well as the local traffic impact of new developments (3.4.5);

- demonstration projects exhibiting the possibilities of high densities of economic activities and households within high-quality urban environments (3.4.6 and 3.4.7); and,

- the definition of priority zones around new transport infrastructures (3.4.8).

Part IV Conclusions

4.1 Introduction

4.1.1 The purpose of this final part of the report is to draw together the main conclusions. Section 4.2 reviews the planning measures relevant to reducing transport emissions for different travel purposes. Section 4.3 highlights areas for further research.

Crucial assumptions underpinning land-use planning policies to reduce transport emissions

4.1.2 The timescales over which planning can impact upon travel demand are long. A large number of factors will influence the emissions efficiency of different transport modes and travel demand. Several important assumptions concerning future changes have underpinned this study and analysis:

- There will be slow improvements in the CO_2-emissions (and energy) efficiency of all modes. Whilst alternatives to the petrol/diesel engined private motor car exist, which have less polluting characteristics - taking account of both manufacture and operation - only relatively gradual improvements in CO_2 efficiencies are likely;

- Telematics and advances in telecommunications are unlikely to reduce significantly the travel demand associated with work activities, although some minor shifts from travel to/from work, to travel within work, are possible. (Indeed it may be that telecommunications will widen the process of economic integration and areas of business interaction, resulting in increases in travel demand);

- Increasing economic integration, specialisation and interdependencies between economic activities will tend to increase total work-related travel; and

- There is a complex relationship between overall travel, congestion and emissions. The differentials in the efficiency of private motor vehicles travelling at different speeds could decrease with improved engine-management systems. If so, any reduction in CO_2 emissions, achieved through reducing congestion and increasing speeds of urban traffic, may become less significant.

Clearly, in so far as the conclusions drawn in this study are sensitive to these assumptions, it will be of considerable benefit to monitor their robustness.

Reducing transport CO2 emissions and other planning objectives

4.1.3 There is a remarkably good general correspondence between most of the broad planning policies that have been pursued in recent decades and the sorts of policies, described more fully below (Section 4.2), that are identified as likely to lead to reductions in travel demand and emissions (Appendix 2). This is all the more noteworthy because very few planning policies have been pursued with the explicit objective of reducing travel demand. The planning policies that are particularly pertinent to the objectives of reducing travel demand are:

- the focusing of development in urban areas;

- the maintenance and revitalisation of local, town and city centres; and

- constraints on the development of new settlements or the extension of "villages" within commuter belts.

4.1.4 In addition, those planning policies which are concerned to improve local environmental conditions and to reduce the local impacts of emissions from transport (noise, CO, NOX etc) are likely to be associated with reductions in overall travel demand and hence CO_2 emissions. Equally, to the extent that the wider policies proposed here to reduce CO_2 emissions are successful, they are likely to reduce the adverse local impacts of transport. Planning policies have also tried to maintain reasonable levels of access to facilities for different socio-economic groups. This objective, too, is likely to be reinforced by the policies put forward here.

4.1.5 At the same time, few planning policies in recent decades have acted to stimulate travel demand. Possible exceptions include Green Belts (Section 2.4), which appear to have extended commuter distances, previous policies of population dispersal and, perhaps, current policies to maintain population in some rural areas.

4.1.6 Planning policies in their role of reconciling competing pressures for land uses, both influence and need to take account of market trends and pressures. Several aspects of recent economic trends and development pressures, themselves in part driven by the low real private costs of motor travel, may inhibit the implementation of the planning policies most likely to encourage reductions in transport emissions. These aspects include:

- Household preferences for low-density housing in rural areas and small towns;

- The decline in the traditional premiums associated with central locations for employment uses and the strong market interest in the development of more peripheral, low-density business parks offering good access by car for employees;

- The extension of choice in the consumption of both private and public services which has for example, been associated with increases in car-borne travel to places of education;

- Strong pressures for the decentralisation of manufacturing as the economies of agglomeration have declined;

- Apparent economies of scale associated with the decentralisation and provision of good access by car, for example, shopping and leisure services. (However, it is interesting in this context that most leisure developments are unable to generate the residual values necessary for the central locations that could reduce associated travel demand); and

- Increasing integration between economic activities in different locations and the demands of modern production and distribution systems, such as just-in-time deliveries.

4.1.7 At the same time, it is evident that in circumstances of low real costs of travel, if the market mechanisms alone allocate sites, then land-use configurations associated with high travel demands are likely. The planning policies suggested in this study are partly based on the view that locations that have exceptional road access should be safeguarded for land uses that actually need these attributes.

Land-use planning as contingency planning

4.1.8 Whilst there has been considerable growth in overall travel demand, travel for different purposes has increased at different rates. There is also evidence that perceptions of the generalised costs of travel may effectively limit the growth in travel demand for particular individuals and purposes. As a corollary of this, however, reduction in travel for a particular purpose may be associated with increases in time and resources spent travelling in pursuit of other activities.[106] Put simply, an individual may not be prepared to spend more than 10 hours per week (or say 10% of income) on travel to work, but a significant reduction in these costs could be associated with an increase in travel for leisure purposes. Certainly, the similarities in the time spent travelling by car-owning and non car-owning households would support this contention.

4.1.9 If this is so, then planning policies may not in themselves lead to marked reductions in travel demand. Planning policies can, however, have a significant and fairly immediate impact on modal choice towards more CO_2-efficient modes for many purposes. More significantly, they can help to create physical environments within which the future need for travel will be lessened.

4.1.10 If the future economic and policy environment increases the generalised cost of travel by CO_2-inefficient modes - through increases in travel costs and congestion, for example - then travel demand will decline. In the meantime planning policies will have helped to create circumstances in which the benefits of access will have been maintained. Thus, in large part, the planning policies suggested below should be viewed as contingency planning, increasing the opportunities for future travel by emissions-efficient modes.

4.2 Planning Measures Relevant to Reducing Travel Demand and Encouraging Shifts to More Emissions-Efficient Modes for Different Purposes

4.2.1 There have been marked changes over time in travel for different purposes and in the use of different modes for these purposes. The potential for planning to influence travel demand for different purposes varies markedly. It is likely to be most influential in relation to travel to work and to have least impact on travel for leisure purposes (Section 1.2). Individual planning measures can be relevant to reducing travel demand for more than one purpose, and the combination of planning measures will be necessary to encourage reductions in transport emissions. Nevertheless, it is helpful to consider the main planning measures relevant to different travel purposes.

Journeys to or from work

4.2.2 Journeys to or from work accounted for 20% of total travel by car in 1985/86. Journey lengths are longer for larger cities, but the possibilities of shifts to more CO_2-efficient modes increase with city size. (Central London is interesting in this context. As described in Section 2.3, the remarkably high spatial concentration of employment in Central London is associated with both long travel-to-work journey lengths and high levels of use of public transport.)

4.2.3 Whilst overall travel-to-work may not increase as quickly as travel demand as a whole in future, the following planning measures will be helpful in encouraging reductions in travel demand:

- the concentration of employment uses in existing centres and other locations well served by public transport (see Appendix 1);
- high-density residential developments concentrated near to transport nodes and in corridors served by public transport (see Appendix 1);

- the release of adequate housing land on suitable sites within urban areas so as to limit constraints on the housing market, and maximise the possibilities for households to locate close to their places of work:
- measures to encourage the use of CO_2-efficient modes, particularly cycling and walking (Section 3.3); and
- constraints over the development of sites with inadequate public transport access for high travel-generating uses (Section 2.4).

Travel within the course of work

4.2.4 The planning policies relevant to reducing travel to work will be, to some degree, helpful in reducing the need to travel within the course of work. Other initiatives which are likely to support such reductions include:

- measures to reinforce urban and city centre regeneration and the juxtaposition of linked economic activities which are not inherently car dependent; and
- road/rail interchange facilities to enable people living or working outside cities to switch from car to rail for long-distance travel.

4.2.5 It should be stressed, however, that planning policies that significantly constrain travel within the course of work could be expected, a priori, to generate significant economic costs. As a corollary of this, reductions in travel demand for other purposes will have the benefit of releasing road capacity for these purposes.

Goods vehicle travel

4.2.6   There is little reason to suppose that planning can have any predictable, significant impact on freight kilometre tonnes moved, and research on freight has not been a major focus of the study. There must, however, be a strong expectation that freight kilometerage is set to increase in importance as a source of transport emissions. Planning does have an important role in keeping open or creating longer-term opportunities to increase the role of modes other than road. Relevant measures include:

- protecting and creating options to service major industrial sites by rail;

- supporting the creation of intermodal freight handling facilities; and

- creating or preserving options for the use of waterways for the movement of freight - particularly aggregates.[107]

Shopping and personal business

4.2.7   The planning policies most pertinent to reducing CO_2 emissions associated with travel for shopping, are those which:

- encourage local convenience shopping;

- maintain and revitalise existing central and suburban shopping centres; and

- encourage in-centre location of large convenience/food stores in district centres.

Travel for social and entertainment purposes

4.2.8   Travel demand for social and entertainment purposes is extremely diverse (Section 1.2). Whilst it is difficult for land-use planning measures easily to influence this source of travel demand, because it is so important (and there may be considerable further scope for growth) even marginal impacts will be of considerable benefit.

4.2.9   Key additional land-use policies which are relevant include:

- central location of certain leisure activities, with suitable public transport access; and

- encouragement of local leisure and entertainment facilities.

Travel for holidays

4.2.10 Travel demand for holidays is perhaps the most difficult for planning policies to influence. Reductions in emissions from travel for this purpose are likely to be best achieved through shifts towards more emissions-efficient means of travel and here planning can have only a modest influence through, for example:

- encouraging the location of new attractions where they are accessible by public transport (2.4.7).

Travel for education, health and other public services

4.2.11 Although constituting only a small proportion of overall travel it has been acknowledged that, as some of this activity - particularly education - takes place in the morning peak period, it has important implications for traffic management. Policies to extend choice in the consumption of public services and to increase financial efficiency in their provision could be associated with increases in travel demand for these purposes. Planning measures could make a significant contribution to reducing transport emissions associated with travel for education and other public services, such as health, by for example:

- ensuring that decisions on the location or relocation of these facilities include considerations of the overall travel demand implications;

- encouraging the provision of educational facilities in parallel with residential development; and

- encouraging design and road configurations that facilitate the use of non-car modes through, for example, improving safety for pedestrians and cyclists, so encouraging parents to allow children to make their own way to and from school (1.2.13).

4.3 Priorities For Further Research

4.3.1 The study has been able to draw upon a wide range of existing research studies. The new evidence assembled has also thrown light on some of the complex relationships that exist between land uses that can be influenced by planning and transport emissions. There remain, however, many areas of uncertainty and the study has had to rely upon data sets which are somewhat out-of-date and in many respects insufficient to illuminate key questions on the relationship between land use and transport emissions. Eleven topics emerge from the study and are put forward below for consideration. These themes relate to both:

- basic research to understand behaviour and trends (topics 1 - 5); and

- research to evaluate the effectiveness and impact of policy measures (topics 6 - 11).

1. The assessment of changes in travel behaviour of individuals and households resulting from changes in the place of residence and place of work

4.3.2 The validity of the study policy conclusions rests upon an assumption that, if planning measures reduce the "need" to travel by car of individuals and households for specific purposes, or encourages travel by emissions-efficient modes, then overall emissions will decline. There is, however, as pointed out above, a concern that time saved through not travelling for one particular purpose (say journey to work) could be offset by increased travel for another (say leisure).

4.3.3 The extent to which such substitution is likely to occur, given any changes which take place in the real costs of travel by private car, and the extent that these are borne financially by the car user, is also highly policy relevant.

4.3.4 Thus, there would be merit in undertaking research that identified (through for example travel diaries) the effects on overall individual/household travel patterns of changes in, for example, the juxtaposition of places of work and home.

4.3.5 Research to explore the likely effects of changes in the costs of travel by different modes on choices over locations for residence and work and travel demand would also be a value.

2. The types of travel demand generated by emergent land uses

4.3.6 The policy conclusions of the study have suggested both that the travel demand (as opposed to traffic generation) characteristics of land uses should be considered at the planning stage and that sites which benefit from good road access should be set aside for land uses that have an apparent "need" for such access. Existing data are poor on the characteristics of the travel demand associated with particular land uses. What does exist tends to focus on the numbers of trips and types of vehicles generated by the land uses. There are, however, evident changes in the characteristics of land uses associated with wider economic, social and technological changes.

4.3.7 There would be merit therefore in further work to examine :

- the total travel demand characteristics (mode, length and frequency of trips attracted) of different types of land uses (for example, business parks, leisure facilities, tourist destinations and public facilities) and the activity-specific and contextual characteristics that influence these ; and

- the extent to which good road access is critical to the competitiveness of different manufacturing and distribution activities. Such research could help inform any adjustments in the Use Class Order that could facilitate planning measures designed to make optimum use (in both economic and transport emissions reduction terms) of sites benefitting from good road access.

As a corollary to this improved data on the travel behaviour of different population groups would also be of value.

3. Research on short-distance trips

4.3.8 It is evident that a high proportion of all trips are short distance and they make a significant contribution to transport emissions not least because motor cars are energy inefficient over short distances. However, there is relatively little data available on personal travel patterns for short-distance trips (<2 km) and the extent to which they can be influenced by planning policies. It would be helpful therefore to improve data availability generally in this area and to undertake focussed research to help assess the contribution that planning policies might make to encourage the use of emissions-efficient modes.

4. Further analyses of the relationship between density, settlement size and regional, urban and neighbourhood structure on transport emissions

4.3.9 The analyses undertaken in this study have been constrained by the dated data, (for example, the last NTS was 1986 and it preceded a period of rapid travel growth), and the limited disaggregations that could be made. More definitive conclusions could be drawn if larger samples of data on travel behaviour were available for a cross section of urban and neighbourhood areas exhibiting distinct characteristics (size, density, structure, etc). For example, it would

be valuable to explore the importance or otherwise of these physical characteristics on travel (and emissions) for particular purposes and the influence of income and car ownership to a greater extent than was possible in this study.

5. Research into the adaptability of planning measures to technological changes affecting transport emissions

4.3.10 As stressed above, the policy conclusions drawn in this study are based upon a number of assumptions, including an assumption that the private petrol/diesel-engined motor car will remain the dominant means of transport (and source of transport emissions). It is worth reflecting that many UK cities had more or less their current structures (size, population, transport infrastructure) in the period before the widespread availability and use of the petrol-engined private motor car. It is possible that the same physical structure will need to respond to the changes brought about by technological development, including the possibilities of emissions-efficient private cars, electric vehicles, and systems of traffic management that increase the utilisation efficiency of road space and new forms of public transport.

4.3.11 Thus, it is critical that independent and balanced assessments of the technological developments are provided for those involved in the development and implementation of relevant planning measures. This will help inform the likely relative impact of planning measures in different localities on transport emissions.

6. Predicting and monitoring the impact of co-ordinated planning and transport strategies on travel demand and on mode choice

4.3.12 The study's policy conclusions have stressed the need for co-ordination between planning and transport policies and infrastructure provision. Such co-ordination appears to have the potential to limit transport emissions to levels substantially less than they would otherwise be. However, the extent to which this is possible is likely to vary between locations.

4.3.13 So far the estimates of the extent of such impacts have been based upon simulations utilising existing transport models rather than longitudinal studies of actual change. There would be benefit in further work in different localities, assessing the likely implications for transport emissions of different levels and locations of development and investments in transport infrastructure. The conclusions of this work could inform local planning policies.

4.3.14 There would also be benefit in monitoring closely the impact of co-ordinated planning and complementary transport policies in localities where explicit policy objectives have been set to reduce transport emissions and where co-ordinated measures are being implemented. Such monitoring would be concerned primarily with the changes in overall transport emissions (or fuel consumption) relative to what would have been expected in the absence of the co-ordinated strategy. Inevitably, concrete results on this criterion would only be available after several years. In the meantime, monitoring of specific measures involving individual policies or combinations of planning and complementary measures (such as parking provision, parking pricing and bus priorities to encourage more transport emissions-efficient shopping) could be undertaken. A critical aspect of such monitoring would be a consideration of the complex interaction between planning, congestion and transport emissions.

7. The long-term development and travel impact of major road and rail projects

4.3.15 As stressed in Section 2.5 the impact of transport infrastructure on development pressures and hence transport emissions is not well understood, not least because of the limited number of ex-post assessments which have been undertaken of major projects in the U.K.. The evidence suggests that the impacts depend upon the planning policy context, the extent and pattern of existing development pressures, the degree to which development has been constrained by problems of accessibility and the local labour market and environmental conditions. If the planning of major infrastructure projects is to take greater account of planning and transport emissions considerations as opposed simply to conventional transport benefits, then there is a need for in-depth, longitudinal, ex-post impact studies.

8. Assessing the implications of intensification and centralisation on travel patterns

4.3.16 The evidence reviewed in the study suggests that intensification and centralisation of activities will encourage reductions in transport emissions through reducing the need to travel and encouraging the use of emission-efficient modes. These relationships could be further explored through ex-ante assessments and longitudinal monitoring studies in areas where these policies have been pursued.

9. Assessing the implication of developing local facilities

4.3.17 The study findings indicate that the availability and quality of local facilities can make a contribution to reducing transport emissions in so far as they encourage short trips and walking and cycling. Many factors affect the viability of local facilities and it would be useful to examine in more detail the extent to which individual and combinations of local facilities can create the conditions to affect transport emissions.

10. Assessing the effects of complementary measures : priority measures for buses, cyclists and pedestrians, parking policies and traffic calming

4.3.18 As has been stressed elsewhere in the report planning policies to reduce transport emissions need to be reinforced by complementary measures. The assessment of such methods have tended to stress the impacts on travel times and local environment and road safety rather than overall transport emissions. There would be value therefore in longitudinal studies (ideally before and after monitoring) that assessed the impact of such measures on the pattern of trip making and mode choice.

11. The effects of locating office and employment uses near to public transport facilities

4.3.19 There is evidence that the location of office and employment uses near to public transport facilities can influence the labour catchment area and the mode choice of employees. However, these effects appear to vary between types of locations (for example central areas of large cities, suburban centres, locations within public transport corridors) and types of office use. It would be useful therefore, to monitor the variations in the factors influencing transport emissions (mode and distance travelled to and from and during work) associated with different types of location and office functions (for example, administration, head offices, local services and international companies).

Appendix 1 Simulations of Alternative Development Patterns

Introduction

1. As part of the study a range of simulations were undertaken of the implications of different patterns of urban growth for total travel demand and, where possible, modal choice and energy consumption and hence CO_2 emissions. These simulations were undertaken for five of the case study areas for which existing strategic transport models were available from earlier studies. The basic approach was to simulate the effects on travel demand of particular levels of housing and employment growth taking place in alternative locations within a specific urban area. Whilst resources did not permit every option to be simulated in each area, analogous simulations were carried out for each type of pattern of urban growth in more than one of the areas to ensure that conclusions did not simply reflect the particular characteristics of individual models and areas.

2. The same models were also used to test the implications for travel demand, modal choice and energy consumption of locating a given quantity of retail floorspace in alternative parts of the urban area, and of alternative locations and types of provision for public services. For the purposes of assessment the work utilises estimates of changes in fuel savings, associated with particular development options, as a proxy for impact on emissions.

3. Such simulations provide a systematic analysis of the way in which particular transport networks would be used by new traffic and the impact on existing movements. The models have been calibrated to reflect observed travel patterns obtained from base year surveys. All of the models are able to predict the numbers and pattern of private vehicle movements within the individual study areas; some are also able to predict public transport usage. Where a modal-choice sub-model is not available, the impact of alternative development scenarios on the distribution of trip lengths provides some indication of the extent to which a switch from private vehicle to other modes of transport, including walking and cycling, might occur under different patterns of urban growth and location options.

4. In each case, the effects on travel demand were limited to the modelled areas and no assessment has been made, for example, of the number of trips that might be attracted into the area by the provision of a new facility. Neither has any attempt been made to assess how intervening opportunities arising from a new development might redistribute existing origins and destinations within the areas. Any additional trips either generated by new developments or arising from a general increase in trip making were assumed to distribute themselves in the same way as existing trips from similar zones. The 'generalised cost' assignment parameters have been held constant between the base and forecast scenarios. The travel demand analyses undertaken for the predominantly urban case study areas have concentrated on peak periods, reflecting the issues which the transport models have been developed to address.

5. Travel demand, as expressed by a trip matrix of journeys between each origin and destination, is allocated to alternative modes, where relevant, and to appropriate routes through each transport network by an assignment process. Separate trip matrices are developed for different trip purposes for each mode and then combined prior to assignment. The assignment of public transport and private vehicle trips is carried out independently.

6. The assignment model uses a predetermined method for selecting the most appropriate routes for each origin and destination pair in the trip matrix. A

journey by public transport, for example, has a number of elements which could influence the route taken, including walk to the stop, waiting time, travel time, interchanges and walk to the final destination. The assignment of private vehicles takes account of the effect of congestion on journey times and the generalised cost of travel. The parameters which determine the routes selected when trips are assigned are developed when the base model is calibrated.

7.   In each case, the simulation study area encompasses the origins and destinations of both existing and generated traffic on all routes. The approach allows existing traffic to modify its route in line with any changes, for example with congestion patterns, resulting from the higher traffic levels.

8.   The pragmatic approach to assessing alternative policy options contrasts with that of other studies designed to compare the potential energy efficiency of various idealised urban forms. It reflects the view that the major practical issues for planning are the implications of alternative patterns of incremental growth for existing settlements.

Alternative Patterns of Growth

9.   Although a range of patterns of growth have been assessed, it is useful to focus on two principal issues:

● the travel implications of alternative patterns of growth in and around essentially freestanding towns and cities; and

● the travel implications of alternative strategies intended to achieve the regeneration of specific metropolitan sub-regions.

(i) Patterns of growth in freestanding towns and cities

10. It is useful to present summary results of two of the key simulations. In both cases the objective of the simulation was to explore the implications of alternative patterns of growth. In neither case was there any attempt to relate assumptions to the level of growth actually anticipated in the areas concerned or to assess the physical feasibility or acceptability on other criteria of the patterns of growth considered. The first simulation considers the implications of locating a 10% growth of population and employment in an urban area with limited existing congestion in the following alternative patterns of growth :

● focusing growth at high density in the existing central area;

● focusing growth along an existing major radial route; and

● a more dispersed, lower density pattern of growth at the periphery of the area which is served by a major orbital road as well as two radial routes.

11. The results indicate that, in terms of distance travelled, total travel demand is greatest with the peripheral expansion option and lowest with the central area expansion option (Table 1.A), although the difference in vehicle kilometres travelled between those options is less than 3%. Because of the improved accessibility to strategic routes serving the whole urban area, the peripheral growth option is associated with the highest average speeds and lowest average journey times. Overall, although the simulation does not provide a formal prediction, the effect on emissions will be fairly similar between the options because the lower journey distances in the centralised options are associated with higher journey times and hence lower vehicle operating efficiencies.

Table 1.A **Travel implications of Town Expansion Options**

		Options					
Travel Implication	Base Case	Central Area Expansion	Ranking	Linear Expansion	Ranking	Peripheral Area Expansion	Ranking
Private Transport							
Vehicle hours	15416	17662	2	18281	3	17374	1
Vehicle kilometres	619760	669703	1	676684	2	688847	3
Average speed (kph)	40	38	2	37	3	40	1
Average Journey length (km)	11.7	11.6	1	11.6	1	11.8	3
Average Journey Time (mins)	17.5	18.4	2	18.9	3	17.8	1
Public Transport							
No. of passenger boardings	17877	19179	1	20084	3	19337	2
Passenger hours	3340	4118	3	4061	2	3743	1
Passenger kilometres	54721	59156	1	60727	3	60279	2
Average journey length (km)	4.1	3.9	1	4.2	2	4.2	2
Average journey time (mins)	15.1	16.3	2	16.7	3	15.8	1
Vehicle kilometres	1974	1974	1	1974	1	1974	1

Note:1. All options, excluding the base case, involve a 10% growth in development.

12. The lower half of Table 1.A presents travel statistics for public transport users under each development option. The number of public transport passengers (in terms of the number of boardings) is highest - as might be expected - for the linear expansion option. Public transport priority measures - such as bus lanes - or new public transport investment are also likely to have the greatest potential to encourage a switch from private to public transport under the linear expansion option because of the concentration of new demand which is created. Equally this concentration of demand in specific corridors has potential implications for the viability of public transport investment and new services.

13. The second simulation assesses the effects of different options for allocating a 5% growth in housing and employment in a freestanding town. The options assessed are:

● extension of existing outer suburbs;

● expansion of existing satellite village settlements;

● focusing growth in a concentric pattern around the inner urban area; and

● focusing growth in a specific inner suburb.

14. The results of the simulation are shown in Table 1.B. The urban infill options involve less distance travelled and are more fuel efficient than the urban extension and expanded village development option, although the differences are in some cases small.

15. The marginally better performance on the distance and fuel consumption criteria of the concentric inner development option compared with more focused inner suburban growth is a consequence of the greater congestion effects of the latter option. Similar simulations in other case study areas produced broadly comparable results. In all cases urban intensification is associated with the lowest average journey distances, journey times and levels of fuel consumption. The simulations, using models allowing for mode choice, also suggest that the relative attractiveness of public transport is marginally greater under the central area and inner suburb expansion options.

16. The simulations generally, therefore, again reinforce the conclusion that concentrated, relatively centralised development options are likely to be more efficient from an emissions perspective than lower density, decentralised, more peripheral patterns of development. However, there is a clear indication, taking the simulations as a group, that the potential benefits are dampened, and could in practice be outweighed, by the rerouting and reduced vehicle operating efficiencies resulting from the increased congestion associated with the former types of option. The transport models which are utilised represent, as noted, peak period conditions and the presumption is that congestion related effects will be much less important in relation to non-journey-to-work travel.

(ii) Urban regeneration

17. The potential significance, from an emissions perspective, of particular land use and transport strategies for urban regeneration has been assessed. Three options have been considered in relation to one metropolitan sub-region:

● a land use policy combining the concentration of commercial development into existing centres and the restriction of growth elsewhere in the sub-region, complemented by balanced investment in public and private transport infrastructure (Option 1);

Table 1.B **Travel implications of Localised Growth Options**

Travel Implications	Base Case	Urban Extension	Ranking	Expanded Village	Ranking	Concentric Inner Area	Ranking	Inner Sub-urban	Ranking
				Options					
Total travel time (hrs)	8067	8164	3	9189	4	8130	2	8105	1
Average time (mins)	19.4	18.7	3	21.0	4	18.6	2	18.5	1
Total travel distance (km)	461389	463795	3	472959	4	461399	1	462915	2
Average distance (km)	18.5	17.7	3	18.0	4	17.6	1	17.6	2
Average Speed (kph)	57.2	56.8	2	51.5	3	56.8	2	57.1	1
Fuel consumption (litres)	4827	5054	3	5190	4	5002	1	5021	2
Total trips (vehicles)	24983	26232		26232		26232		26232	

Notes:1. Fuel consumption is calculated for the urbanised area.
2. All options, excluding the base case, involve a 5% growth in development.

- the creation of a major new urban centre, combined with additional highway capacity and public transport infrastructure investment (Option 2); and

- a third test biased towards extending public transport provision with limited additional highway capacity, combined with the regeneration of existing centres (Option 3).

The main findings are summarised in Table 1.C.

18. Compared to a base do minimum option, all options offer significant benefits. The emissions reductions by the year 2011 vary from 16% in the case of the last option, to 11% for the first option and 9% for the second option. It is also interesting to note that extending public transport provision also provides the best option - although marginally - in terms of minimising journey times for users of both public and private transport. Given the approach taken to the simulation it is not possible to distinguish the relative contributions made by the public transport investment and the land use changes in Option 3.

19. The regeneration of existing centres combined with investment in public transport options offers both somewhat lower journey times and a fairly significant reduction in emission levels. When the first and second options are compared, the policy of regenerating existing centres appears to offer a greater benefit in reducing future emissions than the development of a major new centre within the sub-region. Differences in the quality of travel - measured in terms of journey times and speeds - are, however, in most cases small.

Table 1.C **Pollution, vehicle speed and journey time consequence of urban regeneration options**

	2011 Do Minimum	Option 1	Ranking	Option 2	Ranking	Option 3	Ranking
Air Pollution Indices[1] (Average for all Districts)	100	89	2	91	3	84	1
Vehicle Speeds (kph)[2]							
Peak Hour							
Area A	16	18	1=	17	3	18	1=
Area B	19	22	2	21	3	23	1
Area C	12	15	1	13	3	14	2
Area D	12	14	1=	13	3	14	1=
Off Peak Hour							
Area A	27	29	1	27	2=	27	2=
Area B	35	38	1	37	2=	37	2=
Area C	19	26	1	19	2=	19	2=
Area D	21	23	1	22	2	21	3
Journey Times (minutes)[3]							
Private Vehicles							
Area A	39	38	2=	38	2=	36	1
Area B	28	25	2=	25	2=	24	1
Area C	47	41	1	45	3	43	2
Area D	34	33	3	32	2	31	1
Public Transport							
Area A	63	54	2=	54	2=	53	1
Area B	54	49	2=	49	2=	48	1
Area C	68	59	3	54	2	49	1
Area D	54	41	3	40	2	39	1

Notes: 1. Index of air pollution resulting from private vehicles, per unit area, based on peak hour traffic flows and speeds.
2. Average private vehicle speed (kilometres per hour) in each Area for all trips exclusive of motorway links.
3. Peak hour home based work trip weighted average journey time (minutes) from home to employment.

Appendix 2 The Assessment of Land-Use Planning Measures

Introduction

1. This Appendix provides an assessment of the following land-use planning measures which have been identified as likely to contribute to a reduction in travel demand:

- the intensification of development within existing urban areas;

- the expansion of settlement on public transport nodes and in transport corridors within areas of restraint such as green belts;

- the development of new dense settlements with planned populations in excess of 25,000;

- constraints on housing development in rural areas;

- increases in densities of new housing development in urban areas;

- increases of employment densities and the intensification of development at nodes on the public transport network;

- increases in the intermixing of land uses;

- restrictions over the use of sites with good road access; and

- the concentration of retail facilities in existing urban centres.

2. For each of these measures the following questions have been addressed:

(i) what are the likely impacts of the planning measures on aspects of travel demand (journey frequency, patterns, length etc), and on modal choice and, thus, on CO_2 emissions?

(ii) how far does this impact depend on other supportive policies, or how might other policies enhance or risk negating the favourable impact?

(iii) what type of implications does the measure have for other publicly-borne costs?

(iv) what are the implications of the measure in terms of the range of impacts on different groups?

(v) what are the major risks and uncertainties involved?

(vi) what, if any, implications does the measure have for the achievement of planning and other public policy objectives?

Each of the measures identified above is discussed in turn.

The intensification of development in existing urban areas

3. Such measures include restrictions on the extension of urban boundaries and the enabling of high-density employment and residential development and redevelopment.

(i) Impacts on travel demand and modal choice

4. For sizeable urban areas these measures are, in general terms, likely to maintain or increase existing population and employment densities, contributing to reductions in overall travel demand. This will be reinforced through their effect in enhancing the vi-

bility of public transport and opportunities for walking.

(ii) Dependence upon supportive policies

5.   To be successful it will be necessary for households and employment uses to be persuaded to trade off space for the benefits of accessibility. Their willingness to do so is likely to depend upon the character of the urban area and quality of life factors. Supportive policies would include :

- the provision of high-quality urban green space and entertainment facilities;
- improvement in public transport; and
- enhancing opportunities for walking and cycling.

(iii) Implications for other publicly-borne costs

6.   There will be potential savings in the costs of providing new physical and social infrastructure outside existing urban areas. In so far as the costs of development of infrastructure within the urban area may be high, because of the difficulties of land assembly, costs of reclamation and land values influenced by "hope" and institutional factors, some additional publicly-borne costs may occur.[108]

(iv) Impacts on different groups

7.   There are two areas of possible detrimental impact :

- a)   intensification could result in congestion, loss of amenity and a deterioration in the quality of life for those living in urban areas; and

- b)   constraints on housing land availability in non-urban areas could limit access to affordable housing for those living in non-urban areas.

Against this, the opportunities for improving the accessibility of urban residents, and particularly those without access to cars, are good.

(v) Major risks and uncertainties

8.   There is some risk that, if intensification measures are applied insensitively and not supported by complementary measures, increases in congestion could occur. In the absence of marked improvements in vehicle efficiency, this would result in an increase in emissions. It is clearly important that account is taken of such risks and measures are taken to encourage modal shifts.

9.   In so far as such measures may limit the locations available for employment uses, economic costs could arise. Such risks could be minimised by ensuring that employment uses with a high dependency on road access, particularly for the delivery of goods, assume some priority for sites offering good road access. Secondly, policies should encourage the concentration of high-density employment uses in locations with good public transport access.

(vi) Implications for planning and other public policy objectives

10.   The intensification of development in urban areas is consistent with the thrust of planning policy in the post-war period. It is likely to further objectives to regenerate urban areas, protect the countryside from urban encroachment and to recycle derelict and underused land. However, its success will depend upon the extent to which it is implemented so as not to compromise the quality of the urban environment, and perceptions of the desirability of urban areas as places within which to live and work.

The expansion of settlements at public transport nodes and in transport corridors within areas of restraint such as green belts

11.   Such a planning measure would involve the selective expansion of urban areas and new settlements at high densities in locations affording good public transport access.

(i) Impact on travel demand and modal choice

12.   The levels of impact will be dependent upon particular local circumstances. Overall travel demand will be reduced most where settlements and developments assume a scale above which reasonable levels of self containment for journeys to work obtain and where high densities enable the use of emissions-efficient modes for other journey purposes.

(ii) Dependence upon supportive policies

13. The link with public transport provision and particularly rail transport is particularly critical.

(iii) Implications for other publicly-borne costs

14. These are likely to be minimised if the developments are substantial and/or if they take place close to existing urban areas.[109]

(iv) Impacts on different groups

15. Such measures may benefit both lower-income groups seeking housing within areas of restraint and economic activities wishing to locate on well-accessed sites with good access to a local labour force. A corollary of a selective relaxation of restraint policies would probably be a tightening of constraints elsewhere. This would tend to limit housing movements in these areas, benefiting those owning property and disadvantaging those seeking to enter the market.

(v) Major risks and uncertainties.

16. To implement such measures would require a high level of strategic direction and control.

(vi) Implications for planning and other public policy objectives.

17. There are two main potential policy conflicts. The first concerns the impact on land take and, if primacy is given to public transport access in the planning of developments beyond existing urban boundaries, then environmental concerns, such as landscape value, might receive less priority. However, the concentration of development at relatively high densities should ultimately be preferable for both land-take and visual impact. The second concerns the possible detrimental impact on urban regeneration and indeed on the measures put forward above to intensify development in existing urban areas. There is clearly a question of balance and the need for the expansion of existing settlements will be confined to localities and regions experiencing significant growth so as not to "divert" development pressures beneficial to urban regeneration.

The development of new, dense settlements with planned populations in excess of 25,000

18. In circumstances when growth at the regional level cannot satisfactorily be accommodated through the two measures outlined above, then the development of substantial new settlements could be appropriate.

(i) Impacts on travel demand and modal choice

19. Settlements relatively isolated and in excess of 25,000 population have the potential to attain a strong measure of self containment in journeys to work and enable the provision of viable public transport systems, both for strategic access and local movements. The overall impact on travel demand will, however, be a function of size, social structure, facilities and transport infrastructure provided, as well as distance from major centres.

(ii) Dependence on supportive policies

20. The viability of such developments is likely to depend upon the consistency of the strategic planning framework and the primacy given to design and layout factors that encourage reductions in travel demand.

(iii) Implications for other publicly-borne costs

21. It is likely that high levels of public investment in infrastructure would be required if settlements of this scale are to be created. However, in circumstances of high growth, this investment would lead to significant financial returns and could well involve lower costs than a wider dispersal option. It would be necessary to explore these considerations through scenario studies.

(iv) Impacts on different groups

22. Such measures could be of particular value to non-car owning households, providing satisfactory design and land-use arrangements and public transport facilities are incorporated. The most significant costs would fall on those wishing to live in areas of restraint.

(v) Major risks and uncertainties

23. The risks are twofold:

- car ownership levels could be high and such settlements could, particularly in circumstances of low real transport costs, afford good access to the countryside and strategic road networks. There could be increases in travel for social, entertainment and holiday purposes in particular; and

- if growth rates at the regional level are less than anticipated, such planned dispersal could jeopardise urban regeneration policies.

(vi) Implications for planning and other public policy objectives

24. In broad terms such measures would be consistent with existing planning policies, providing that they did not lead to inappropriate incursions into the countryside and constrain the development of smaller settlements, particularly isolated settlements whose viability was already threatened. The circumstances in which such measures are likely to become appropriate are unlikely be widespread in the UK.

Constraints on housing development in rural areas

25. This measure would comprise restraints on the release of housing land in small - less than 3,000 population - settlements, particularly those within the hinterland of major urban settlements, which have in recent years have tended to attract car-borne commuters.

(i) Impacts on travel demand and modal split

26. Settlements of less than 3,000 population tend to generate high levels of travel per capita and long trip distances for both work and non-work journeys. Whilst only a minority of the population live in such areas, significant reductions in travel demand could be attained through some constraint on their further development.

(ii) Dependence on supportive policies

27. If such constraints are to be acceptable it will be crucial to ensure that sufficient opportunities to accommodate growth exist elsewhere.

(iii) Implications for other publicly-borne costs

28. These are unlikely to be very significant, although some savings in infrastructure costs could occur.

(iv) Impacts on different groups

29. There is some likelihood of costs being imposed on households seeking to enter the housing markets in the rural areas subject to constraint. At the same time existing house owners in these areas could benefit from the policy.

(v) Major risks and uncertainties

30. Such constraints could hamper policies designed to ensure balanced development and maintenance of population in rural areas.

(vi) Implications for planning and other public policy objectives

31. By and large this measure would be consistent with planning policies, except in so far as in remote rural areas (where some population decline may occur) the policy could be in conflict with development objectives. Planning policies have tended in the past to spread development amongst settlements. This approach would require a stronger measure of intervention to focus development in particular settlements.

Increases in densities of new housing development in urban areas

32. Such planning measures could encourage non-traditional forms of housing development (for example, terraced town houses with underground parking of cars for occasional use, and well-serviced apartment blocks close to public transport).

(i) Impacts on travel demand and modal choice

33. National Travel Survey data indicate that people living at low density travel almost twice as far (and twice as often) as people living in high-density areas. The differences are even more striking if only travel by car is considered. Depending upon the particular circumstances, the measures should both help reduce travel demand; enhance the viability of public transport; and encourage cycling and walking.

(ii) Dependence upon supportive policies

34. To achieve success it will be necessary for households to be willing to trade space for improved accessibility. The measure will also depend upon the effectiveness of other policies aimed at improving the quality of the urban environment. Such policies include the provision and maintenance of green space and high design standards. The measure would need to be supported by appropriate transport infrastructure and constraints on housing developments in non-urban areas.

(iii) Implications for other publicly-borne costs

35. There may be savings in the costs of provision of new social and physical infrastructure elsewhere. At the same time intensification will put pressure on existing urban infrastructure, where renewal is required the costs could be high.

(iv) Impacts on different groups

36. Such a planning measure might arguably better suit the needs and aspirations of small and single person households than families with growing children, as the availability of space for private gardens would be limited. However, the former are the most rapidly expanding household types.

(v) Majors risks and uncertainties

37. There is some likelihood of increased localised congestion. However, this in itself is likely to encourage some shifts from motorised to non-motorised modes. The major uncertainty rests with whether sufficient numbers of households would be willing to accept higher-density urban living.

(vi) Implications for planning and other public policy objectives

38. The measure is consistent with urban regeneration and countryside protection policies. However, there have also been policies to limit housing densities which would need to be revised in some areas.

Increases of employment densities and the intensification of development at nodes on the public transport network

39. Such measures would involve the concentration of employment and other uses (leisure, retail etc) at key nodes on the public transport network, particularly the rail network.

(i) Impacts on travel demand and modal choice

40. The main impact of the policies on transport emissions would be through an encouragement of the use of emissions-efficient modes rather than to encourage a reduction in travel demand.

(ii) Dependence on supportive policies

41. The measure could be supported by car parking controls and improvements in public transport service levels and quality. Close integration of planning and transport infrastructure measures would be essential.

(iii) Implications for other publicly-borne costs

42. Such measures would improve the viability of public transport services.

(iv) Impacts on different groups

43. Households and employers located close to public transport networks would be significant beneficiaries.

(v) Major risks and uncertainties

44. There are no major risks. The level of impact will depend upon the effectiveness of supportive policies and the quality of developments achieved relative to market demands. The effectiveness of implementation will depend upon a strong measure of control over developments.

(vi) Implications for planning and other policy objectives

45. The measure is broadly supportive of other planning policies. It could enhance the viability of existing and potential new rail services.

Increasing the intermixing of land uses

46. Such a measure would benefit from the general improvements in the good neighbour quality of employment uses. However, it should not involve a general "scattering" of land uses.

(i) Impact on travel demand and modal choice

47. These are difficult to predict and the impact is unlikely to be marked in circumstances of low energy prices. However, it could help contribute to the development of "urban villages" within which trips are characteristically short and possible to make by emissions-efficient modes, particularly walking and cycling.

(ii) Dependence on supportive policies

48. Policies designed to encourage urban intensification and to increase the density of new housing development would complement the measures for increasing the intermixing of land uses. Mixed uses could be encouraged by ensuring large redevelopment schemes include residential, shopping and recreational uses. It may also be possible to retain existing non-commercial uses within central areas through the extension of measures which protect open space, historic buildings and certain shop frontages and also by encouraging the restoration of residential uses on upper floors, whilst retaining commercial uses on the ground floor. Traffic calming measures and limitations on car access could reduce congestion and the negative externalities associated with the greater intermixing of uses.

(iii) Implications for other publicly-borne costs

49. None are apparent.

(iv) Impacts on different groups

50. Providing care is taken to ensure the continuing segregation of "bad neighbour" uses, the overall impacts are likely to be favourable. Increasing the intermixing of land uses could improve the quality of the urban environment by creating a diverse pattern of land use and enabling people who so wish to live close to work places and services they require on a daily basis. This will help create a built environment which encourages social interaction, improves security, reduces the need for car usage and also reduces the need for commuting from residential suburbs.

51. Important and complex linkages exist between labour and housing markets. Increasing the intermixing of land uses might be expected to benefit people who have a low level of mobility and increase female participation rates. In many cases, the job choice by a lower-earning partner will follow, rather than determine, household residential choice. This is particularly the case if the lower-earning partner's employment is part-time, since the number of hours worked has been shown to be a major determinant of the travel time of employees.[110]

(v) Major risks and uncertainties

52. Increasing the intermixing of land uses raises the potential for savings in travel demand. Whether or not this happens is likely to depend on the availability and relative attractiveness of public transport and the design features of the particular development in question. There is a danger that, without an accompanying modal shift, pedestrian and vehicular conflicts would increase and the quality of the urban environment would deteriorate, possibly increasing the pressure for decentralisation.

(vi) Implications for planning and other policy objectives

53. There may be some conflict with planning concerns over removing non-conforming uses. However, the policy might contribute to the achievement of a variety of other public policy objectives, including discouraging crime; improving the efficiency of urban labour markets through increasing participation rates; and encouraging flexible employment practices.

Restrictions over the uses of sites with good road, rail or water access

54. The measure would involve restricting the uses of sites with good road, rail or water access to uses with high trip-generation characteristics for journeys other than car journeys to work (ie. freight). These uses would include, for road and rail, some manufacturing and distribution activities while, for water, uses would involve bulky goods, such as aggregates, minerals and oil. Those uses most likely to be associated with high travel demand and emissions from car journeys to work are office and business uses with high employment densities. In order to achieve such a restriction a strong measure of public control over land uses would be helpful. (A corollary of this measure could be restrictions on the uses of sites with poor public transport access, particularly for office uses.)

(i) Impacts on travel demand and modal choice

55. The location of "goods intensive" firms on the periphery of urban areas close to the main inter-urban road network could help reduce congestion and improve environmental quality in urban centres. Retaining service and employment-intensive activities in central locations would enhance the possibilities for modal shifts from private motor vehicles.[111]

(ii) Dependence on supportive policies

56. The feasibility of the measure is likely to require consistent policies at the regional level to prevent the use of car accessibility as an instrument of competition between areas. The location of labour and visitor-intensive activities at locations easily accessible by public transport services would require the improvement of public transit systems.

(iii) Implications for other publicly-borne costs

57. Complementary policies to improve public transport systems could be associated with high costs.

(iv) Impacts on different groups

58. The measure could benefit households without access to a car by increasing the number of job oppor-tunities which are accessible by public transport. There may also be significant implications for economic efficiency:

- the measure might ease labour-market shortages by concentrating labour-intensive activities in central locations at public transport nodes; and
- it could "crowd out" lower value-added industry on the fringe of central areas.

(v) Major risks and uncertainties

59. These predominantly concern market trends and impacts on the efficiency of economic activities. Also, local planning authorities may not be willing to trade-off possible short-term economic/employment gains for the reductions in car travel.

(vi) Implications for planning and other public policy objectives

60. The policy is compatible with a range of other public policy objectives, particularly urban regeneration and improving accessibility to job opportunities.

The Concentration of Retail Facilities in Existing Urban Centres (City and district/suburban centres)

61. Such policies would include limitations over the development of retail facilities outside existing urban centres and the maintenance and development of hierarchies of centres.

(i) Impacts on travel demand and modal choice

62. Concentrating retail facilities in existing centres - in preference to out-of-town centres - will, by raising the density of trip ends, help support public transport services and increase the possibility for making multi-purpose trips. Town centre locations for retail activities, as illustrated by the simulations, also generate more trips of a relatively short length, which increases the potential for some modal shift to walking/cycling.

(ii) Dependence on supportive policies

63. Supportive measures to strengthen existing centres include: concentrating major new 'comparison' shopping and leisure complexes on city-centre sites; upgrading existing shopping streets through environmental improvements and, where possible, creating weather-proof arcades; improving traffic control and management with the aim of producing pedestrianised areas and improving the flow of traffic around urban centres; improving access by public transport; permitting some limited decentralisation - particularly of heavy car-borne shopping activities - to suburban locations which will help reduce traffic congestion in centres; and, combining park-and-ride facilities with superstores in urban/city centre fringe locations to ensure the viability of town centres for "comparison" shopping.

(iii) Implications for other publicly-borne costs

64. The measure should: help ensure use of existing infrastructure; help improve the viability of public transport; and improve the commercial and economic viability of town centres. This could both help further physical conservation and encourage tourist and visitor activity.

(iv) Impacts on different groups

65. Concentrating facilities in existing urban areas should increase accessibility by public transport to the benefit of non-car owning groups and low-income households. More generally, it benefits the consumer, through emphasising the role of competition and choice between adjacent shops. It also provides the convenience of making a variety of purchases and using service facilities in a single trip.

(v) Major risks and uncertainties

66. In the absence of suitable remedial measures, concentrating developments in central locations could exacerbate traffic congestion and pedestrian/vehicular conflict. Congestion has complex effects on trip patterns and there is the risk that failure to control congestion might increase travel demand and add to the pressure for decentralisation to uncontrolled locations. Given changes in consumer behaviour and the increase in bulk buying, there are circumstances where a certain amount of permitted decentralisation to suburban locations could help reduce town-centre congestion and - where another superstore already exists - may also help reduce car journey distances for food shopping.[112] However, case study evidence indicates that shopping centres located near orbital routes are more difficult to serve efficiently by public transport. The simulations further suggest that orbital/bypass locations are associated with higher private vehicle travel distances/times and levels of fuel consumption relative to alternative suburban or central locations.

(vi) Implications for planning and other policy objectives

67. The general thrust of the policy would support objectives to improve accessibility and town centre viability. There is the possibility of some conflict in certain circumstances with urban regeneration objectives, where the relative mobility of investments in shopping developments are seen as a cornerstone of urban regeneration in some areas outside of existing centres.

Appendix 3 Case Study Areas

REGION	SUB-REGION/URBAN	NEIGHBOURHOOD
South East	Central London	
	Croydon	
	Greenwich	Lakedale Vanburgh
East Midlands	Derby	
West Midlands	Black Country	Bilston North Bilston East Charlemont St. Pauls
	Coventry	
	Shrewsbury	Cherry Orchard Sutton Farm
North West	Birkenhead	
	Runcorn	

H

Appendix 4 Statistical Analyses of Determinants of Travel Demand

Introduction

1. The analysis is based upon National Travel Survey (NTS) cross-section data for the 11 Standard Planning Regions for 1978/79 (subsequently referred to as 1979) and 1985/86 (subsequently referred to as 1986). Data are available for average distance travelled per person per week for work and non-work journeys by car, public transport, walking and other means.

The influence of car ownership, employment in services and urbanisation on work related travel

2. Table 4.A summarises the preferred equations, which are those standard linear regressions which provide the best fit using the ordinary least squares minimisation criterion. Since the relationships for 1979 and 1986 turn out to be rather similar the explanations for the 1986 results are stressed.

3. The variables considered 'explain' some 54% of the variation between regions in total work related travel in 1979, although rather less (40%) in 1986. Distance travelled for work is strongly related to car ownership - particularly ownership of two cars. Obviously here the direction of causality may be two way; long journeys to work and high car ownership may both be related to occupational factors. The co-efficient just fails the standard 5% significance test but markedly improves the performance of the equation. Percentage employment in services also, has a

positive impact on distance travelled. In neither case is the co-efficient significant at the 5% level but in both instances the inclusion of the variable markedly improves the performance of the equation.

4. The percentage of work related travel is in both cases positively related to ownership of one car - although in 1986 the co-efficient was not significant at the 5% level - and is strongly, negatively related to percentage employment in services. The percentage of travel-to-work by public transport equation performs particularly well. Use of public transport is negatively related to ownership of one car (although the co-efficient is not significant) and positively related, as expected, to percentage employment in services and level of urbanisation (or population density).

5. The percentage of travel-to-work by walking equation fits well in 1979 with walking negatively related to car ownership. However, this relationship largely breaks down in 1986 as indicated by the low R-bar-squared figure. It might be speculated that this is related to the decline in manufacturing in areas where walk to work has been traditional. The failure of density or urbanisation to figure as an explanation is noteworthy.

The influence of car ownership and settlement size on travel

6. The analysis here concentrates on 1986 for which 14 observations are available (rather than the 12 available for 1979) for the following 14 urban areas: Inner London; Outer London; West Midlands; Greater Manchester; West Yorkshire; Glasgow; Liverpool; Tyneside; Other urban areas with a popu-

Table 4.A Factors influencing work related travel 1979 and 1986.

Dependents	All Journeys 1979	1986	% by Car 1979	1986	% by Public Transport 1979	1986	% Walk 1979	1986
Explanatory Variable								
CONSTANT	-84.69 **(-0.6)**	-286.92 **(1.1)**	60.54 (3.6)	92.65 (3.0)	4.65 **(0.4)**	-22.95 **(-1.7)**	3.30 (8.3)	1.40 (5.8)
% owning 1 car			0.62 (2.3)	0.31 **(1.3)**	-0.37 **(-1.9)**	0.19 **(-1.3)**	-0.03 (-4.8)	
% owning 2 cars	6.62 (2.8)	6.79 **(2.2)**					-0.03 **(-1.9)**	
% employed in services	5.01 **(1.4)**	8.40 **(1.3)**	-1.03 (-2.4)	-1.12 (-3.7)	0.97 (2.3)	1.17 (3.72)		
Level of Urbanisation					0.23 (2.3)	0.15 **(2.0)**		
R-bar-squared	0.543	0.398	0.384	0.463	0.782	0.841	0.682	0.200
Standard error of regression	57.50	73.46	6.65	5.83	4.53	3.59	0.192	0.198
Fsc	0.75	0.04	0.55	0.82	0.03	3.22	0.33	0.10
F_{FF}	0.65	0.69	2.64	0.59	0.58	0.89	0.09	0.04
X^2	0.63	0.43	0.70	1.32	1.16	0.56	1.28	1.03
FH	1.79	5.01	0.02	0.01	0.37	0.20	0.02	1.25

Notes: 1. Approximate critical values at the 5% level are: t-tests - 2.3, (figures in bold indicate non-significant t ratios)
2. Diagnostic Tests (FSC, Fff, X2) - 5.99; (FH) - 5.2

Table 4.B The influence of settlement size on work related travel (1986)

	All Journeys	Percent by Car	Percent by Public Transport	Percent by Walk
Explanatory Variables				
Constant	-77.15 **(-1.1)**	49.54 (5.7)	27.97 (3.6)	2.31 (5.7)
Car Ownership	9.02 (7.6)	0.30 **(2.0)**	-0.22) **(-1.6**	-0.02 (-2.9)
Urban Size	0.000018 **(1.6)**	-0.0000014 **(-1.7)**	0.0000033 (2.5)	
R-bar-squared	0.813	0.313	0.390	0.372
Standard error of regression	54.07	6.86	6.17	0.34
Fsc	0.27	0.45	3.13	0.53
F_{FF}	0.17	0.22	0.60	4.17
X^2_N	0.93	0.92	0.46	0.44
F_H	0.77	3.96	**8.76**	3.55

Notes: 1. Approximate critical values at the 5% level are: t-tests - 2.3, (figures in bold indicate non-significant t tests).
2. Diagnostic Tests (FSC, Fff, X2) - 5.99; (FH) in 5.2

Table 4.C **The influence of settlement size on non-work related travel**

Non-Work Journey Equations.

Dependents	All Journeys 1986	% by Car 1986	% by Pc. Tpt. 1986	% walk 1986
Explanatory Variable				
Constant	171.19 **(1.4)**	35.66 (10.3)	31.43 (9.4)	6.55 (6.2)
Car Ownership	15.21 (6.7)	0.61 (9.7)	-0.47 (-6.4)	-0.07 (-3.5)
Urban Size			0.00000070 **(1.3)**	
R-bar-squared	0.770	0.877	0.771	0.458
standard error of regression	105.17	2.91	3.34	0.89
Fsc	0.44	0.28	1.11	0.92
F_{FF}	0.75	0.02	1.40	0.004
X^2	1.00	0.61	2.41	0.60
F_H	0.01	2.14	2.08	**9.392**

Notes: 1. Approximate critical values at the 5% level are: t-tests - 2.3, (figures in bold indicate non-significant t tests).
2. Diagnostic Tests (FSC, Fff, X2) - 5.99;(FH) in 5.2

lation over 250,000; and for areas of population size: 100,000-250,000; 50,000-100,000; 25,000-50,000; 3,000-25,000 and rural (taken to represent areas with a population of less than 3,000). For the purpose of the analysis the population of each urban area and type of settlement is taken to be the mid point of the quoted range.

7. Because the non-metropolitan country areas cannot be specifically identified the range of potential explanatory variables is effectively limited to car ownership (available from the NTS database - in this case ownership of one car) and population size.

8. The regression results are summarised in Tables 4.B and 4.C Car ownership has a powerful effect on

extent of work related travel and has some - although this is not at the 5% level always statistically significant - effect on use of car, public transport and walk. Population size has some apparent positive effect on distance travelled and there is some tendency for use of public transport to increase with urban size, although again the relationship is weak.

9. For non-work travel car ownership has a clear, powerful effect on distance travelled and a strong negative effect on use of public transport and walk. There is some weak tendency for greater use of public transport in larger urban areas. Interestingly, although urban size has a significant negative effect on non-work travel in the 1979 equation although, this had disappeared by 1986.

Notes And References

1. *This Common Inheritance: Britain's Environmental Strategy, Environment White Paper, 1990.*

2. Climate Change 1992: The Supplementary report to the Intergovernmental Panel on Climate Change, Cambridge University Press, 1992.

3. The figures from the National Travel Survey only relate to those trips which are 1.6 kms or greater in length. This means that walking trips are underestimated in the data.

4. Hazel G. *What Traffic Impact?* Report to the Institution of Highways and Transportation Conference on the Impact of Major Developments, 1988.

5. The Department of Employment, *Leisure Day Visits Survey*, HMSO: London, 1991.

6. Hillman M, Adams J & Whitelegg J, *Children's Independent Mobility*, PTRC Conference, University of Sussex, 9-13 September, 1991.

7. Kenworthy J and Newman P, *Cities and Automobile Dependence*, Gower Technical: Aldershot, 1989.

For further comparisons of travel demand in Europe see Department of Transport, International Comparisons of Transport Statistics, HMSO: London, 1991.

9. Department of Transport Statistics 1990 show that road vehicles per thousand population in the UK at 407 per thousand were lower than in many other EC countries - former Federal Republic of Germany (534), France (524), Italy (582), Luxembourg (490), Netherlands (432) - and substantially lower than the figure for the United States (823).

10. Department of Energy. *Digest of UK Energy Statistics.* HMSO: London, 1990.

11. Fergusson M, Holman C and Barrett M. *Atmospheric Emissions from the Use of Transport in the UK: Volume One; The Estimation of Future Emissions*, Godalming, 1989; and Fergusson, M and Holman C. *Volume 2: The Effect of Alternative Transport Policies,* Godalming, 1990.

12. Fielding T & Halford S. *Patterns and Processes of Urban Change in the United Kingdom*, London: HMSO, 1991.

8. *Table 1* **Passenger transport per head of population by mode for selected European countries (1990)**

	GDP £ per head of population	Cars and Taxis	Public Transport[1]	All Modes
Great Britain	9,566[2]	10,586	1,412	11,997
Belgium	11,008	7,622	1,681	9,303
Germany (Former FDR)	13,365	9,388	1,594	10,982
France	11,879	10,413	1,862	12,274
Italy	10,634	8,555	2,260	10,815
Netherlands	10,552	8,992	1,623	10,614
Sweden	15,004	10,071	1,764	11,835

Source: Department of Transport. Transport Statistics Great Britain 1992. London: HMSO
Notes: (1) Includes buses, coaches and rail transport, but excludes metro.
(2) UK figure.

13. Hall, P, *Urban and Regional Planning*, Penguin Books; Middlesex, 1975.

14. Halcrow Fox and Associates/Birkbeck College, University of London, *Investigating Population Change in Small to Medium Sized Urban Areas*, London: DOE, 1986.

15. Johnston R & Gardiner V, *The Changing Geography of the UK*, Routledge: London, 1991.

16. Wakeley, N, 'Work, Rest and Play', *Estates Gazette*, June 22, 1991.

17. West Midlands Joint Data Team, *Planning Trends in the West Midlands*, JDT: Solihull, 1991.

18. Massey D, *Spatial Divisions of Labour: Social Structures and the Geography of Production,* London: Macmillan, 1984.

19. Scott, A.J. and Storper M, High Technology Industry and Regional Development, *International Social Science Journal*, No. 112, 1987. Also see Schoenburger E, `Technological and Organisational change in the Automobile Production: Spatial Implications: *Regional Studies*, Vol. 21: No. 3, 1987.

20. Fothergill S & Gudgin G, *Unequal Growth: Urban Regional Employment Change in the UK*, Heinemann: London, 1982.

21. Rajan A, `Services: `The Second Industrial Revolution`, London: Butterworth, 1987.

22. Jones Lang Wootton, *The Decentralisation of Offices from Central London*, JLW: London, 1990.

23. The proportion of households with no cars between 1978 and 1988 fell from 43% to 35%. Over the same period the proportion of households owning one or more cars rose from 57% to 65% with a substantial increase in the proportion of households with 2+ cars; from 12% to 21%.

24. Labour Force Surveys show activity rates for women aged between 25 and 49 experienced an annual growth rate of 2.39% from 1983 to 1989.

25. Kitamura R, *Lifestyle and Travel Demand* in Transport Research Board 'A Look Ahead: Year 2020, NRC: Washington, 1988.

26. ibid.

27. NRTF forecasts forecast a lower rate of growth in car ownership in future years. Car traffic is predicted to increase by 142% in the high growth scenario between 1989 and 2025; this level of growth was achieved in the 22 years previous to 1989. The annual growth rate in female activity rates is also predicted to fall below 2% in the period up to the end of the century.

28. Department of the Environment, Planning Research Programme, *Land Use Planning and Climate Change*, HMSO: London, 1992.

29. Climate Change 1992: The Supplementary report to the Intergovernmental Panel on Climate Change, Cambridge University Press, 1992.

30. *Energy Policy Implications of the Greenhouse Effect, Sixth Report, Energy Committee of the House of Commons*, Volume I, report and proceedings, HMSO: London, 1989.

31. Department of the Environment, *Digest of Environmental Protection and Water Statistics*, No 13, DoE, HMSO, 1990.

32. Transnet, *Energy, Transport and the Environment,* Transnet: London, 1990.

33. ibid.

34. ibid.

35. Kenworthy J and Newman P, *Cities and Automobile Dependence*, Gower: Aldershot, 1989.

36. Steadman P and Barrett M, *The Potential Role of Town and Country Planning in Reducing Carbon Dioxide Emissions*, The Open University, 1990.

37. Some time budget studies suggest that car-owning and non-car owning households tend to spend roughly the same amount of time on travel per week, indicating that people do not spend money to save time on travel, but rather devote the same time travelling further by faster modes. See for example Goodwin P, *Travel Choice & Time Budgets,* PTRC Paper No.142.

38. ibid.

39. At the international level the key research is that by Kenworthy and Newman (1989) noted in reference 35 above. In the UK a comprehensive analysis of the relationship between travel demand and density is provided by Hillman and Whalley (1983). The results of their analysis of the National Travel Survey are illustrated in Table 2, note 51 below.

40. The results of the regression analyses are shown and commented on in Table 1 of Appendix 4.

41. The Influence of Density on Travel Behaviour.

The following equations were derived from multiple regression analysis. Each equation given below takes the form of :

$$Y = a + bx_i + Cx_{ii}$$

The elements of the equation comprise Y, which is equivalent to distance travelled (the dependent variable); Xi and Xii which are the elements used in the regression analysis to try to explain the variation in the dependent variable (Y); and the co-efficients a, b and c which are constants determined by the analysis to link the three variables (Y, Xi, Xii) by a linear equation. This equation can be used for predicting the value of Y for known values of Xi and Xii.

The overall strength of the equation is given by R^2 (co-efficient of determination). R^2 lies between 0 and 1, the nearer R^2 is to 1, the better the explanatory performance of the equation. An R^2 of 0 indicates no relationship between the dependent (Y) and explanatory variables (X_i, X_{ii}).

The direction of the relationship between Y and each X variable is denoted by the sign (-/+) of the constants b and c. The figures immediately below the constants are test statistics (t ratios) which are compared to table values to determine how significant each coefficient is. Figures in bold indicate coefficients which are not statistically significant.

Thus, the first example given below in 41(i) indicates that for each extra percentage owning one car, average distances travelled for non-work journeys will increase by 15.28 kms per person per week, (assuming population density remains constant). Similarly, if population density increases by 1 person per hectare, then average distance travelled for non-work journeys will decrease by 0.03 kms per person per week (assuming percentage ownership of one car remains constant).

R^2 in the 34(i) is 0.759, which implies that 75% of the variation in the dependent variable (distance travelled) can be explained by the equation. However, the emboldened t ratio for population density indicates this variable has no statistically significant effect on this equation.

All of the equations below, including those given in notes 35 to 37, 49 and 50, follow the same format and thus can be interpreted in the same manner.

41(i) The preferred equations, t ratios in parentheses, are:

Average distance travelled for non-work journeys (standard planning region) for 1979 =

266.12   +15.22 (POOL)   - 0.03 (PD)
(1.8)   (5.6)   (-1.6)
$R^2 = 0.759$

Percentage of non-work journeys by walking (standard planning regions) for 1986 =

6.22   -0.06 (POOL)   + 0.001 (PD)
(6.9)   (-4.1)   **(1.5)**
$R^2 = 0.614$

42.   The preferred equation for 1985/6, is:

Average distance travelled to work (urban case study areas) =

3.79   + 0.11 (PES)   -0.0048 (PD)
(3.1)   (4.2)   (-2.5)
$R^2 = 0.670$

43.   The equation is:

Total travel by car (urban case study areas) =

-482.2   + 90.3 (CO)   -0.68 (PD)
(-0.2) **(1.7)**   (-2.8)
$R^2 = 0.55$

44.   The equation is:

Percentage travel to work by public transport (urban case study areas) =

-4.64   + 0.42 (PES)   + 0.0050 (PD)
(-0.9) (3.9)   (6.4)
$R^2 = 0.832$

List of Abbreviations

POOL - Percentage ownership of one car

PD   - Population density

PES   - Percentage employment in services

CO   - Car ownership

45.   Hillman M and Whalley A, *Energy and Personal Travel: Obstacles to Conservation. PSI: London, 1983.* See also the Report of the International Collaborative Study of the Factors Affecting Public Patronage, *The Demand for Public Transport*, TRRL: Crawthorne.

46.   Kenworthy J and Newman P, *Cities and Automobile Dependence*, Gower Technical: Aldershot, 1989.

47.   For example, Transportation Planning Associates and ECOTEC, *Black Country Integrated Transport Strategy*. TPA: Birmingham, 1990.

48.   The results of the regression analysis are shown and commented on in Tables 2 and 3 of Appendix 4.

49.   There is a substantial correlation between PU and PD ($r_2 = 0.9$) and, although this is less severe than at the regional level, both variables cannot appear in the same equation. There is also some degree of multicollinearity ($r_2 = c0.4$) between these variables and population size. This may account for the failure of population size to figure in any of the preferred equations. As most of the case study areas are not free-standing towns the concept of population size for these areas is arguably anyway misleading.

50.   Maltby D, Monteath I G & Lawler K A 'The UK Surface Passenger Transport Sector: Energy Consumption and Policy Options for Conservation' *Energy Policy,* December, 1978.

51. *Table 2* **Settlement Size and Personal Travel (1979)**

	Distance travelled each week (kms)				
	per person all methods	per person car travel	per car	No. of car journeys per person per week	average length of car journey (kms)
Rural areas	194	150	258	11	13.2
Small towns	167	124	260	10	13.0
Medium towns	146	99	234	9	10.9
Cities	144	98	228	9	11.3
Within cities, areas of:					
low/med density	156	110	238	10	11.3
high density	124	76	205	7	10.9
Conurbations	133	82	215	8	10.9
Within conurbations areas of:					
low/med density	148	101	233	9	11.1
high density	117	64	191	6	10.9

Source: Hillman M & Whalley A. Energy and Personal Travel: Obstacles to Conservation, PSI: London, 1983.

52. Banister R, 'Travel Patterns in South Oxfordshire' in University of Reading and David Lock Associates *Alternative Development Patterns - New Settlements,* DOE: London, 1991.

53. Rickaby P A, Six Settlement Patterns Compared. *Environment and Planning* 13, Vol. 14, 1987.

54. Creswell P and Thomas R, 'Employment and Population Balance' in Evans A (ed) *New Towns; The British Experience,* TCPA: London, 1972.

55. SIC divisions 8 - banking and financial services and division 9 - other services - are used as a proxy for centralisation.

56(a). The equations given below follow the same format to those explained in note 34 above.

Measures of centralisation: work travel.

The preferred equation for 1985/86, t ratios in parentheses, is:

Average distance travelled to work per week =

-286.92 + 6.79 (POTC) + 8.40 (PES)
(1.1) (2.2) (1.3)
$R^2 = 0.398.$

(b). The equation is:

Percentage of work travel by car

= 93 + 0.31 (POOTC) - 1.12 (PES)
(1.3) (-3.7)
$R^2 = 0.463.$

(c). The equation is:

Percentage of work travel by public transport

= -23 + 0.19 (POOTC) + 1.17 (PES) + 0.15 (PD)
(-1.7) **(-1.3)** (3.7) (2.0)
$R^2 = 0.841.$

57(a). Measures of centralisation: non-work travel.

The preferred equation is:

Percentage of travel by car = 5.9 + 0.23 (POOTC)
(6.3) **(1.4)**

+ 0.77 (POTC) - 0.32 (PES)
(2.5) (2.5)
$R^2 = 0.89.$

(b). The preferred equation is:

Percentage of travel by public transport
= 26 - 0.52 (POOC) + 0.45 (PES)
(4.57) (-8.0) (4.5)
$R^2 = 0.89.$

List of Abbreviations

POTC   -   Percentage owning two cars

PES   -   Percentage in services employment

POOTC   -   Percentage owning at least one car

PD   -   Population density

58. The correlation between the developments is 0.7 which indicates a strong statistical relationship between parking availability and proportion of employees using a car to travel-to-work.

59. Dasgupta M, Frost M and Spence N, *Mode Choice in Travel to Work in British Cities 1971-1981.*

Research Papers, Department of Geography: LSE, 1989; Dasgupta et al. *Journey-to-Work Trends in British Cities, 1971-1981.* Research Papers. Department of Geography: LSE. 1990; and Dasgupta et al., *Employment Patterns and Travel Distances in British Cities 1981*, Research Papers, Department of Geography: LSE, 1990.

60. Thomson MJ, *Great Cities and Their Traffic*, Penguin: Middlesex, 1977.

61. Owens S, *Energy Conscious Planning*, CPRE: London, 1991.

62. Tegner G, *Work Trip Patterns in the year 2000 in Six Different Intra-regional Structures*, Stockholm County Council, 1976.

63. ibid.

64. McCarthy R, *Leisure and Retailing; a case study of Meadowhall*, paper given at conference on Britain in 2010: Future patterns of shopping, held by Royal Society of Arts in London 22 June 1989. See also TPA and ECOTEC, *Black Country Integrated Transport Strategy,* TPA: Birmingham, 1990.

65. Kamali F, *Trip Patterns in Newly Created Commercial Centres,* 19th Summer Annual PTRC Meeting. University of Sussex, 9-13 September, 1991.

66. Vincent RA, Layfield RE and Bardsley MD, *Runcorn Busway Study,* TRRL: Berkshire, 1976.

67. Roberts J and Rawcliffe P, *'Fission or Fusion?',* 19th Summer Annual PTRC Meeting. University of Sussex, 9-13 September, 1991.

68. Mitchell C and Stokes R, *Walking as a Mode of Transport,* TRRL: Berkshire, 1982.

69. See also, Hass-Klau., (ed), 'New Ways of Managing Traffic', *Built Environment,* Vol. 12, Nos. 1/10, 1986; Hass-Klau, C., (ed), *New Life for City Centres,* Anglo-German Foundation, London, 1988; and Keller, H.H., 'Three Generations of Traffic Calming in the Federal Republic' in proceedings of Seminar F, European Planning and Transport of the PTRC, 17th *Summer Annual Meeting,* PTRC Education and Research Services, London, 1989.

70. OECD, *Special Research Group on Pedestrian Safety.* OECD: Paris, 1977.

71. Bocking, Bocker and Hass Klau, *The Safety of Cycling in German and British Towns,* PTRC 19th Summer Annual Meeting, University of Sussex, 9-13 September, 1991. See also Tight M R and Carston O M J, *Problems for Vulnerable Road Users in Great Britain, The Netherlands and Sweden,* Institute for Transport Studies: Leeds, 1989.

72. Breheny MJ, 'Towards Sustainable Urban Development', in Mannion A and Bowlby S, *Environmental Issues in the 1990s,* Open University Press; London, 1990.

73. Coopers & Lybrand, *Study of the Basingstoke TTWA,* HMSO: London, 1988.

74. ibid.

75. ibid.

76. ECOTEC and MVA, *Impact of Railway Electrification on House Prices*, ECOTEC: Birmingham, 1990.

77. University of Newcastle-Upon-Tyne, *The Longer Term Effects of the Tyne and Wear Metro,* TRRL: Berkshire, 1990.

78. The modelling approach is based upon regression analysis in which movements in house prices from building society data for the area of impact are 'explained' by movements in house prices in control areas and dummy variable which take on different values before and after the improvements concerned. The sign and significance of the co-efficient on the dummy variable then provides a measure of the effect of the improvement on relative house prices in the area of impact.

79. The modelling approach adopted is explained in note 70 above. The statistically significant variables are indicated by one or two asterisks depending on the level of significance.

Sample Regressions

(t-ratios in parentheses)

St. Albans: 1976-85

DPSTALB = 0.0596 CON + 0.7291 DPSE + 0.1128 DUM78
                (2.3037)*   (3.9928)**   (2.0574)*

$R^2 = 0.7664$.

Luton: 1976-85

DPLUTON = 0.0123 CON + 1.0350 DPSE + 0.1007 DUM78
                 (0.31125)   (3.4752)**   (1.1264)

$R^2 = 0.6782$.

DPLUTON = 0.0370 CON + 0.6143 DPSE +0.1634 DUM7879
                 (1.0427)   (2.7690)**   (2.2876)*

$R^2 = 0.7825$.

Bedford: 1976-85

DPBEDFO = 0.0485 CON + 0.8745 DPSE + 0.0959 DUM78
                 (1.1786)   (3.0143)**   (1.1017)

$R^2 = 0.6210$.

Ipswich: 1984-89

DPIPSWI = 0.0736 CON + 1.3619 DPEA + 0.0848 DUM8788
                (-1.0070)   (2.4925)*   (0.8886)

$R^2 = 0.6101$.

Tonbridge - Hastings

Rother: 1984-89

$$DPROTER = 0.00001\ CON + 0.8191\ DPSE + 0.2119\ DUM8687$$
$$(0.002) \qquad (1.7281)$$

$$(3.4218)$$

$\underline{R^2 = 0.8772}.$

Worcester: 1981-89

$$DPWORCE = 0.0191\ CON + 0.9644\ DPWM + 0.1853\ DUM8387$$
$$(0.3280) \qquad (2.2940)^* \qquad (2.0122)^*$$

$\underline{R^2 = 0.6443}.$

*   Significant at the 90% level
** Significant at the 95% level

List of Abbreviations

DP   -   Change in Prices

DPSE   -   Change in Prices in the South East Exl. Greater London

DPWM -   Change in Prices in the West Midlands

DPEA   -   Change in Prices in East Anglia

80. Krëibich V, `The Successful Transportation System and the Regional Planning Problem: An Evaluation of the Munich Rapid Transit System`. *Transportation*. Vol. 7, 1978.

81. Gentlemen et al., *The Glasgow Rail Impact Study*, TRRL: Berkshire, 1983. See also Anas. A. 'The Impact of Transit Investment on Housing Values: A Simulation Experiment', *Environment and Planning A*, Vol. 11, 1979.

82. University of Newcastle-Upon-Tyne, *The Longer Term Effects of the Tyne and Wear Metro*, TRRL: Berkshire, 1990.

83. Chu C, *Mass Transit Railways and Workplace Location* MSc thesis; Cranfield Institute of Technology, 1979.

84. For an overview see ECOTEC, *Midland Metro Line One; Information for Presentation to Key Developers,* ECOTEC: Birmingham, 1991. and *The Demand for Public Transport,* TRRL: Berkshire, 1980.

85. See for example references 69-76.

86. Leitch G, *Report of the Advisory Committee on Trunk Road Assessment,* HMSO: London, 1977.

87. Grieco MS, *The Impact of Transport Investment Projects Upon the Inner City,* Transport Studies Unit, University of Oxford, 1988.

88. See *Estate Times*, Survey, 1991, op cit and *Estates Gazette* 'Focus on M40 Corridor', September 28, 1991 and Millar D. 'Motorway Blessing', *Estate Times,* Survey: M40 Corridor, November 15 1991.

89. Coopers and Lybrand, 1988, op cit.

90. West Midlands Joint Data Team, *Planning Trends in the West Midlands*, JDT: Solihull, 1991.

91. Mackie A, *Effect of Bypasses on Town Development and Land Use*, TRRL; Berkshire, 1982.

92. Hallet S, *Drivers' Attitudes to Driving, Cars and Traffic - Anaylsis of The Results of a National Survey,* Transport Studies Unit, Oxford University, 1990.

93. Wootton Jeffreys Consultants, *Parking Policies and Standards,* London Planning Advisory Council, 1991.

94. Dryden KR, *Travel Patterns of Office Employees in Central Croydon,* MSc in Transport Planning and Management, Polytechnic of Central London, 1991.

95. Department of Transport, *Park and Ride.* Presented at the English Historic Towns Form Seminar, Oxford, 18th September 1991. See also Oxford City Council *Park and Ride in Oxford.* Presented at the English Historic Towns Form Seminar, Oxford, 18th September 1991; and Holt S and Homer K. *A Review of Park and Ride in the West Midlands*, TPA: Birmingham, 1990.

96. Oxford City Council, *Park and Ride in Oxford,* Department of Engineering and Recreation: Oxford, 1991.

97. Russel J and Pharoah T, *Speed Management and the Role of Traffic Calming in Road Safety*, Heriot Watt University: Edinburgh, 1990.

98. Roberts J, *Quality Streets*, TEST: London, 1988. See also Roberts J, *The European Experience* Royal Society of Arts Conference Paper, London, 22nd April 1987.

99. Elkin T, McLaren D & Hillman M, *Reviving the City: Towards Sustainable Urban Development,* Friends of the Earth: London, 1991.

100. Department of Transport, *Transport Statistics Great Britain 1979-1989*, HMSO; London, 1990.

101. Hudson M, *The Bicycle Planning Book*, Friends of the Earth; London, 1978. Also see Hillman M

and Whalley A, 1983, op cit.

102. Report of the International Collaborative Study of the Factors Affecting Public Transport Patronage, 1980, Op Cit.

103. Rowell A and Fergusson M, *Bikes not Fumes*, CTC: Godalming, 1991.

104. Department of Transport, *Memorandum submitted to the Transport Select Committee on Cycling,* HMSO: London, 8th May 1991.

105. ibid.

106. Goodwin P, op cit, (see reference 37).

107   Currently disused facilities can be safeguarded under arrangements described in paragraph 5.35 of PPG12. For a more detailed discussion of these issues see ECOTEC Research and Consulting Limited, *The Role of Land Use Planning in Encouraging Waterborne Freight,* ECOTEC: Birmingham (Report to the Department of Transport).

108. University of Reading and David Lock Associates, *Alternative Development Patterns - New Settlements,* HMSO: London, 1993. (Forthcoming).

109. Conran Roche, Davis Langdon and Everest Consultancy Group. *Costs of Residential Development*, Conran Roche: London, 1989.

110. Dawson J, Findlay AM and Sparkes L, Defining the Local Labour Market: An Application of Log-Linear Modelling to the Analysis of Labour Catchment Areas, *Environment and Planning.* Vol 18, 1986.

111. See for example, Ministry of Housing, Physical Planning and Environment, *The Right Business in the Right Place*, National Physical Planning Agency: The Hague, 1991.

112. Stokes G, *Research into the Alteration of Travel Patterns Following the Opening of New Superstores - Evidence from a Household Survey in Swindon*, Transport Studies Unit: University of Oxford, 1992.

Printed by HMSO, Edinburgh Press
Dd 0296700 C9 10/93 (215723)